UNLOCKING THE
WISDOM OF LARGE
LANGUAGE MODELS
An Introduction to The Path to
Artificial General Intelligence
EDWARD Y CHANG

Unlocking the Wisdom of Large Language Models

An Introduction to Multi-LLM Agent Collaborative Intelligence

Third Edition

Edward Y. Chang

Computer Science
Stanford University

Preface

This booklet, "Unlocking the Wisdom of Large Language Models (LLMs)", introduces the comprehensive volume "Multi-LLM Agent Collaborative Intelligence: The Path to Artificial General Intelligence" [1, 2]. Through fourteen carefully crafted aphorisms, it distills the foundational insights behind **Multi-LLM Agent Collaborative Intelligence** (**MACI**), a framework proposed as a promising path toward realizing **Artificial General Intelligence** (**AGI**).

In addition to these aphorisms, the booklet includes titles, abstracts, and introductions from the main chapters of the book, along with the full content of Chapter 1.

What follows is the original preface of "Multi-LLM Collaborative Intelligence: The Path to Artificial General Intelligence," which sets the stage for the journey ahead. We are pleased to announce the third edition of the book. This update features significant additions: Chapters 11 and 12 introduce ALAS and SagaLLM, two systems designed to overcome key limitations in long-lived reasoning workflows. These new chapters directly address critical challenges in AI systems: Gödelian barriers to self-validation, context narrowing during extended operations, and the absence of transaction guarantees with persistent memory.

Although critics continue to question whether LLMs can achieve AGI, often citing limitations in memory, planning, and grounding, we offer concrete architectural responses. MACI, especially when instantiated through multi-agent, multimodal collaboration, provides a systemic design that directly addresses these concerns. Frameworks such as SocraSynth, EVINCE, and CRIT, along with our modules for consciousness modeling and behavioral regulation, show how structured interaction, guided by institutional principles and distributed between executive, legislative, and judicial roles, can yield reasoning capacities that no single model could achieve alone. With the addition of ALAS for adaptive planning and SagaLLM for persistent memory, MACI now confronts two of the most enduring objections to AGI: the need for self-verification and the challenge of maintaining the state over time.

Through structured dialogue and role-based specialization, MACI enables LLMs to complement each other, revealing insights that would remain hidden in isolated models. This collaborative dynamic mirrors the success of human institutions, where diverse viewpoints and structured deliberation are essential to progress.

Looking ahead, we envision even more powerful synergies. One LLM may serve as a world-model builder, mapping conceptual relationships; another as a high-resolution sensor, interpreting data streams beyond human perception. Working together, such agents could jointly model and perceive reality in ways that exceed individual human capabilities, opening new epistemic and scientific frontiers.

Whether this architecture ultimately leads to AGI remains to be seen. But we are convinced that intelligence, like progress, does not come from isolation but from cooperation. Similarly, as collective intelligence has driven human advancement, collaborative LLMs can unlock capabilities and insights that no single model can reach alone, transforming how we address the world's most complex challenges.

Edward Y. Chang,
August 15th, 2024.
October 28th, 2024 (second edition).
April 15th, 2025 (third edition).
Series π 0020131G003

Preface to "LLM Collaborative Intelligence: The Path to Artificial General Intelligence"

As Generative AI transforms our world, experts predict the emergence of Artificial General Intelligence (AGI) as early as 2040. This book proposes that the key to achieving AGI, characterized by versatility, adaptability, reasoning, critical thinking, planning, and ethical alignment, lies not in creating more powerful individual models, but in enabling large language models (LLMs) to engage in intelligent and collaborative dialogue. This concept, termed **Multi-LLM Agent Collaborative Intelligence** (MACI) forms the foundation of our exploration.

MACI transcends conventional "mixture of experts" models or traditional LLM debates by optimizing the exchange of information between LLM agents through seven essential foundations.

1. **Balancing Exploration and Exploitation**: MACI takes advantage of various perspectives while maintaining robust reasoning rooted in the strong priors of next-token maximum likelihood predictions. This ensures the exploration of novel perspectives while preserving the stability of the model parameters learned from the training data. (Chapters 6 and 7)

2. **Modulating Linguistic Behavior**: Beyond balancing exploration and exploitation, MACI dynamically modulates the linguistic behaviors of LLM agents, facilitating transitions between contention and collaboration. By fostering productive perspective exchanges quantified through information theory metrics, MACI generates diverse viewpoints and novel insights. Calibrating debate contentiousness enables MACI to explore a broader spectrum of ideas while consistently converging on well-reasoned conclusions. Beyond contentiousness modulation, MACI detects

and regulates behavior across multiple dimensions, including hate speech and empathy, anxiety and calmness, and emotional extremes—ensuring discussions remain productive and ethical while preserving cognitive diversity. (Chapters 9 and 10)

3. **Checks and Balances for Context-Sensitive Ethical Alignment**: Individual LLM agents are assigned specialized roles: the Executive for knowledge formation, the Legislative for developing ethical frameworks, and the Judicial for contextual evaluation. This governance structure allows ethics to be legislated while enabling context-dependent interpretation by the judicial branch. The parameters of the executive LLMs remain unchanged to preserve performance integrity. (Chapter 10)

4. **Persistent Memory as Essential Infrastructure**: LLM agents require persistent memory systems that transcend their limited context windows. Without robust state persistence, agents cannot reliably maintain awareness of constraints, track system states, or execute complex workflows. Even sophisticated validation logic fails without complete historical context, and transaction patterns become meaningless when systems cannot accurately recall previous states. Persistent memory forms the critical foundation upon which both effective validation and reliable transaction guarantees must be built, enabling agents to operate coherently across extended temporal sequences. (Chapters 11 and 12)

5. **Reasoning with the Socratic Method**: MACI employs the Socratic Method to refine reasoning through iterative questioning and dialogue. This approach fosters deeper analysis, challenges assumptions, and enables the discovery of robust solutions by encouraging critical thinking among agents. (Chapter 5)

6. **Frontier Discovery through Polydisciplinary Synthesis**: LLMs are trained without informing the transformer algorithms about document domains. LLM training treats all documents as sequences of words, resulting in representations without domain boundaries where all fields are combined in one unified space. This polydisciplinary representation provides an unprecedented opportunity to synthesize knowledge across traditional boundaries and explore uncharted intellectual territories. It is at these intersections of previously isolated domains that true ingenious intelligence emerges, revolutionizing our understanding and unleashing unprecedented capabilities. (Chapter 15)

Building on these foundations, the fifteen chapters guide the reader systematically from theoretical frameworks to practical applications. Key algorithms include CRIT for critical evaluation, SocraSynth for dynamic dialogues, EVINCE to optimize the flow of information through Bayesian statistics and information theory, SagaLLM to implement persistent memory systems that enable robust validation and preservation of transaction properties, and polydisciplinary synthesis to explore knowledge across traditional boundaries. We explore applications ranging from medical diagnosis to news debiasing and address fundamental challenges in AI safety through checks and balances applied across LLM's linguistic, legislative, and judicial modules, ensuring alignment between knowledge, ethics, and contextual reasoning.

Reframing LLMs as Components in the Path to AGI

Some pioneers of modern AI, including Yann LeCun, argue that LLMs alone cannot achieve AGI due to several fundamental limitations: their lack of persistent memory, reasoning and planning capabilities, and physical grounding. LeCun specifically asserts that true intelligence requires interaction with the physical world through sensors and embodiment. He emphasizes that while LLMs demonstrate impressive linguistic capabilities, they lack genuine understanding and even suggests that "the sensory-motor abilities of a cat surpass those of an LLM." This perspective raises legitimate concerns about current LLM architectures, particularly regarding the efficiency with which humans learn complex skills from few examples, something current systems struggle to replicate. In this book, we reframe this debate by examining how LLMs might serve not as standalone AGI systems but as crucial components within a more comprehensive architecture.

Reframing LLMs' Role in Intelligence Rather than viewing LLMs as standalone forms of artificial general intelligence, we propose reframing them as foundational components within a broader intelligent system. In biological intelligence, consciousness operates on top of an extensive underlying architecture of neural processes (the unconscious) responsible for perception, motor control, memory consolidation, and other essential life functions.

Similarly, LLMs can function as *cognitive substrate* within a modular intelligence framework, responsible for processing, pattern matching, and information synthesis. The external modules can then manage reasoning, validation, planning, and behavior modulation. Although not identical to human unconsciousness, LLMs exhibit functionally analogous capabilities: recognizing patterns, forming associations, and constructing representations that support more sophisticated conscious operations when properly structured.

Critically, this reframing highlights a profound parallel: Human intelligence does not begin as a blank slate. Infants enter the world equipped with evolutionarily encoded unconscious mechanisms that govern breathing, metabolism, coordination, and even basic social instincts. Conscious learning through few-shot experiences and fine-tuning emerges upon this biological foundation. Therefore, comparing an infant's intelligence directly to an LLM is misleading; the infant benefits from billions of years of embedded evolutionary knowledge. Likewise, LLMs provide *artificial unconsciousness*, a foundation on which modular systems can develop structured, adaptive, and goal-directed intelligence. (Chapter 13 provides an in-depth discussion.)

Addressing the Grounding Problem The claim that LLMs lack a world model stems from a particular interpretation of what constitutes "grounding" in intelligence. We support Ilya Sutskever's perspective that documents themselves encapsulate worldviews, and history is fundamentally written in text. Text represents a projection of the world, a distillation of human experience, observation, and reasoning encoded in language.

When LLMs train on vast corpora, they learn to compress and represent the processes that generate these texts. This compression captures significant aspects of human understanding, including causal relationships, physical properties, and social dynamics. Although this text-based grounding differs from sensorimotor grounding, it represents a valuable form of knowledge acquisition that should not be dismissed.

That said, we acknowledge that multimodal perception provides complementary forms of grounding that can enhance an AI system's understanding. Rather than viewing sensory input as the exclusive basis for intelligence, we see it as one of multiple channels through which a system can build comprehensive world models.

The Memory Challenge Current LLMs face two distinct memory-related challenges: context window limitations during inference and the lack of persistent memory between interactions. The first constrains how much information an LLM can consider at once, while the second prevents the accumulation of experience over time. Context window expansions have addressed some limitations, but issues surrounding context loss and context narrowing have caused unexpected inconsistencies in long-lived transactions or long chains of thoughts. Persistent memory integration remains crucial for capabilities like constraint validation, state tracking for action rollback, and maintaining consistency across complex workflows. The SagaLLM framework introduced in Chapter 12 specifically addresses these challenges by adapting saga-transaction mechanisms from database systems to manage memory in LLM-based agents.

SagaLLM enables selective storage and retrieval of critical information (not all memory), maintaining a minimal structured record of past states, actions, and their consequences. This allows for a precise rollback when errors occur and ensures that interdependent processes maintain consistency. In our experiments with planning scenarios such as the Thanksgiving dinner coordination problem, SagaLLM successfully maintained awareness of constraints that the standalone LLMs lost track of during extended reasoning.

Reasoning and Planning Capabilities Building on these memory advances, we now address the significant challenges LLMs face with reasoning and planning in complex, multi-step processes. Although persistent memory provides the foundation, effective reasoning requires additional architectural innovations. The MACI framework leverages SagaLLM's memory capabilities while integrating specialized modules for different cognitive functions. By distributing reasoning across structured components, analogous to the executive, legislative, and judicial branches of government, MACI implements logical operations of checks and balances. This structure supports an iterative process "think, validate, rethink" where each step is recorded in persistent memory, allowing the system to continuously verify that all constraints are observed throughout the planning sequence.

Evidence from our implementation demonstrates that this architecture successfully maintains global constraints across extended planning horizons, effectively detects and corrects inconsistencies in proposed actions, and seamlessly integrates new information without losing critical context. The system's ability to reference previous states and decisions ensures that constraints established early in the reasoning process remain enforced even as plans become increasingly complex. Although these capabilities do not yet match human-level planning, they establish a promising path toward addressing current limitations through architectural innovation rather than relying solely on scaling existing models.

Synthesis: A Modular Path Forward The path toward more comprehensive artificial intelligence likely involves neither pure LLMs nor a complete abandonment of their capabilities. Instead, we envision a modular architecture in which LLMs serve as powerful semantic processors within a larger system that includes dedicated components for perception, memory management, causal reasoning, and action selection.

This framework addresses LeCun's concerns about embodiment and grounding while leveraging the linguistic strengths of LLMs. By integrating sensor modules, persistent memory systems such as SagaLLM, and specialized reasoning components within the MACI framework, we can build systems that combine the pattern matching capabilities of LLM with the physical interaction and persistent learning that critics rightly identify as essential to intelligence.

Rather than asking whether LLMs alone can achieve AGI, we should ask how their unique capabilities can complement other modalities in building more robust, adaptive, and trustworthy intelligent systems. The frameworks presented in this book offer concrete implementations of this vision, demonstrating how LLMs can serve as foundational components in AI systems that reason effectively, maintain memory consistently, and ground understanding in both language and perception.

The path to AGI through MACI is not a sudden leap but a gradual process of structured integration and collaborative evolution. Just as human civilization advances through the accumulation of shared knowledge and social negotiation, multimodal LLM agents can transcend their individual limitations by working together, each contributing to different modes, perspectives, and roles of reasoning. This book provides the architectural blueprints and theoretical grounding to pursue this path, demonstrating how systems built on foundational substrates can evolve toward human-level reasoning and beyond.

To conclude this exploration, Chapter 15 offers a philosophical synthesis. Fourteen aphorisms are distilled from practical experimentation and long-term research. These aphorisms reflect the core insights of MACI and articulate a new paradigm: one where intelligence is not defined by individual scale, but by the capacity for dialogue, regulation and rational alignment with complexity and uncertainty.

Edward Y. Chang
March 13th, 2024 (first edition)

October 28th, 2024 (second edition)
March 31st, 2025 (third edition for Stanford CS372)
Series π 0020131G006

Contents

1 Aphorisms of LLM Collaborative Intelligence

Introduction

This chapter introduces fourteen aphorisms developed from five years of research into multi-agent Large Language Models (LLMs). These aphorisms explain and justify the foundations of MACI (Multi-LLM Agent Collaborative Intelligence), an architecture that organizes multiple LLMs to support reasoning, planning, and decision-making beyond the capacity of single models. Grounded in philosophical traditions and implemented through modular frameworks introduced earlier, MACI views intelligence as dialogic, evaluative, and regulative. Rather than scaling individual models in isolation, MACI coordinates collaboration across diverse perspectives to enable verifiable and context-aware behavior, offering a potential path toward AGI.

The fourteen aphorisms are organized into four conceptual layers that reflect MACI's development from theoretical insights to practical orchestration. These include foundational concepts about truth and validation (Aphorisms 1–4), system-level design principles (Aphorisms 5–8), collaborative reasoning strategies (Aphorisms 9–12), and emergent intelligence mechanisms (Aphorisms 13–14).

Although grounded in earlier frameworks including CoCoMo [3],

SocraSynth [4], CRIT [5], EVINCE [6], DIKE-ERIS [7], and SagaLLM [8], this chapter refers to them only when illustrative. The focus is on the design philosophy they collectively support: that collaborative intelligence, not isolated pattern generation, is the basis of general intelligence.

Each aphorism encapsulates a principle grounded in empirical system development, from questions about epistemology and bias to applied mechanisms for role assignment, linguistic behavior modulation, and validation. Together, they offer a comprehensive framework for understanding and building multi-agent systems.

The fourteen aphorisms are grouped by conceptual layer, reflecting MACI's progression from theoretical principles to system design and emergent intelligence. Table 1.1 summarizes their organization.

Category	**Aphorisms**
Theoretical Foundations	#1: Truth emerges from perspectives #2: External mirrors enable validation #3: LLMs faking reasoning and feelings, just as we do #4: Foundations and adaptations
System Design	#5: Context transforms capabilities #6: Linguistic behavior reflects intention and emotions #7: Checks and balances ensure adaptive alignment #8: Consciousness filters impulse; MACI governs LLMs
Collaborative Dynamics	#9: The essence of precise questioning #10: Debate strengthens reasoning quality #11: Hallucinations fade under scrutiny #12: Polydisciplinary synthesis expands discovery
Emergent Intelligence	#13: Human heuristics are limited and end-to-end learning shows supremacy #14: AGI emerges through collaborative intelligence

Table 1.1: Organizational Map of the 14 Aphorisms of MACI

Aph. #1: Truth emerges from perspectives

"Outside formal systems, objectivity remains a hard problem; what we pursue instead is reasonableness through multiple perspectives."

Mathematics and logic offer certainty through formal proofs, but most real-world domains, such as medicine, law, and journalism, operate under uncertainty and competing interpretations. In these settings, objective truth is often inaccessible. What we can instead pursue is reasonableness, a standard grounded in coherence, evidence, and comparative judgment.

Philosophical traditions have long wrestled with this challenge. Kant distinguished between phenomena (what we perceive) and noumena (things-in-themselves), underscoring how cognition filters all experience [9]. Nietzsche advances this further through his *philosophy of perspectivism*, arguing that "there are no facts, only interpretations." In his view, all truth claims are inherently tied to particular viewpoints [10].

Thomas Nagel, in his "view from nowhere," provides a critical insight: objectivity is not the elimination of perspective, but rather the capacity to synthesize multiple perspectives into a more impartial whole [11]. This concept is closely aligned with how MACI converges on reasonableness by coordinating perspectival agents. Together, these perspectives suggest that truth emerges not as a static entity to be discovered but as a dynamic process unfolding through the interplay of diverse viewpoints. This view echoes the structure articulated in Hegel's dialectical method[1] [12] (further explored in Aph. #10).

[1] Hegel's dialectical method proceeds through a triadic structure: a *thesis* gives rise to its *antithesis*, and their tension is resolved in a *synthesis* that preserves aspects of both. This dynamic underpins the evolution of thought and understanding.

These philosophical insights have direct implications for practical domains where even the so-called "ground truth" may embed uncertainty or institutional bias. A Johns Hopkins study published in 2023 [13] estimated a 10% misdiagnosis rate in US hospitals, revealing the limits of clinical certainty. Similarly, studies of media bias show how divergent expressions influence public understanding [14].

To navigate these uncertainties, MACI fosters dialogue among diverse reasoning agents. Each agent contributes a different perspective, evaluating or reframing claims. Through structured interaction and principled disagreement, the system refines its understanding. Reasonableness emerges not from any one voice, but from how multiple voices interrogate and support each other, a dialectical process of negotiated understanding rather than definitive truth.

Rather than resolving the philosophical problem of objectivity, MACI recognizes its irresolvability and builds upon it as a structural design principle. Through its internal evaluation methods, the system assesses arguments for coherence, evidentiary grounding, and logical structure, measuring how well each claim withstands scrutiny from alternative perspectives. By treating disagreement as a resource rather than a failure, it moves closer to reasonableness, an ideal more aligned with how humans actually make sense of the world.

Note: This aphorism frames the epistemological basis for MACI; Aph. #10 builds on this by detailing how agentic debate operationalizes dialectical reasoning.

Aph. #2: External mirrors enable validation

"No system can fully validate its own reasoning from within, a fundamental limitation shared by monolithic LLMs and human minds, as Gödel's incompleteness theorems reveal."

Both humans and machines face a core limitation: we struggle to detect our own errors. People often miss inconsistencies or typos in their own writing, but spot them easily in others'. Language models face a similar challenge. When operating in isolation, a model cannot reliably assess the soundness of its own output.

This challenge has technical underpinnings. Researchers have identified that the stochastic nature of next-token prediction, conditioned on evolving context, can lead to degradation in reasoning quality. Effects such as effective long-context loss [15], attention narrowing and distraction [16], and context override through state transitions [17] can cause the model to diverge from earlier logic or contradict prior statements without awareness. Without an external reference point, these failures often go uncorrected.

This limitation is mirrored in foundational theories. Gödel's incompleteness theorems show that complex systems cannot establish all truths from within themselves [18]. Wittgenstein emphasized that meaning arises from public language practices, not internal solipsism [19]. And Popper noted that science advances through external falsification, not internal confirmation [20].

Together, these insights point to a common conclusion: Validation requires independence. Sound reasoning is rarely self-contained. It emerges from critique, comparison, and testing across different viewpoints.

MACI addresses this constraint through a distributed validation system. Rather than relying on self-consistency, MACI enables agents to serve as external mirrors for each other. Each model contributes both its own judgment and its evaluation of others. Reasoning becomes more stable and accountable when multiple agents examine claims from independent points of view.

Progress in AI may depend less on increasing internal complexity and more on structuring systems that can challenge, reflect, and revise through collaboration. MACI provides the architecture to support this, making validation not a post-processing step, but an integral function of interaction.

Attaining greater intelligence may not require larger models, but better mirrors.

Aph. #3: Simulated reasoning can be useful, even if not real

"An actor may not feel true sorrow when portraying grief, yet their performance can still move us. The question is not whether the emotion is real, but whether it functions in context."

Language models do not reason or feel the way humans do. They have no subjective experience, emotional memory, or intent. Yet they can often produce outputs that appear reasoned or emotionally expressive. This gap, between form and inner state, raises important questions about what it means to simulate intelligence.

Turing's 1950 formulation suggested that indistinguishability in conversation might be sufficient to attribute intelligence [21]. Although this view has been criticized, most notably by Searle's Chinese Room argument, it nevertheless shifted the focus to behavior over internal structure. In practice, the utility of a system often depends not on how it works internally but on how its outputs function in a broader interaction.

The analogy to acting serves to illustrate this distinction. A skilled actor does not experience the grief that they portray, yet their performance may be compelling and meaningful. Of course, actors draw on lived emotional experience and possess intentionality. LLMs do not. The analogy holds not in terms of internal motivation but in how we evaluate the product of a performance: by its coherence, appropriateness, and effect.

Likewise, Erving Goffman's theory of social performance described how people change roles based on context and audience expectations [22]. Humans adapt strategically and with awareness. LLMs lack such metacognitive control. But their outputs can still be modulated to adopt different roles, such as analyst, critic, or teacher.

This is where MACI provides architectural clarity. It does not treat LLMs as conscious agents. Instead, it uses their capacity for simulated role enactment within a structured environment. Roles are assigned, perspectives are coordinated, and outputs are checked by other agents. This process does not generate genuine understanding, but can still support useful reasoning behavior when mediated by architectural safeguards.

Simulation, in this view, is not deception if it is constrained, transparent, and subject to verification. MACI's purpose is not to pass as human, but to leverage the expressive potential of LLMs in a way that supports deliberation, critique, and adaptive planning.

Treating simulated reasoning as real reasoning would be a mistake. But rejecting simulation outright would ignore its functional value, especially when structured through external moderation and multi-agent feedback. MACI acknowledges this distinction and builds on it. The intelligence that emerges is not located in any one model, but in the interaction between them.

Aph. #4: Foundations and adaptations

"Intelligence operates on dual layers: a data-intensive foundation akin to unconscious processes and an agile contextual layer resembling conscious adaptation."

Critics often note that LLMs require vast amounts of training data, while humans can learn from only a few examples. Yet, this contrast obscures a deeper structural parallel: both biological and artificial intelligence operate across two interdependent layers, one foundational, the other adaptive.

In humans, the foundational layer includes perceptual and emotional responses shaped by evolution and habit. Freud describes this as the unconscious mind, a reservoir of impulses beneath awareness [23, 24]. Kahneman reframes this as "system 1" thinking: fast, automatic, and intuitive [25]. When reflection is needed, humans engage "system 2," in a slower, deliberative process capable of overriding instinct and reasoning through complexity.

Similarly, LLMs are trained on massive corpora to build a statistical foundation of linguistic fluency. This enables rapid generation in familiar contexts. However, when faced with novel questions, ambiguity, or conflicting interpretations, models cannot rely solely on their internal training. Their behavior must be shaped externally, through validation, feedback, role constraints, or collaborative feedback.

MACI does not introduce a third layer, but formalizes and activates the adaptation layer through structured, multi-agent coordination. It adds mechanisms for critique, counterargument, and revision, not by modifying weights but by orchestrating interaction among agents with complementary roles. Through moderated dialogue and perspective shifting, MACI constructs a deliberative framework atop static foundation models.

This dual-layer design helps resolve the apparent contradiction between data-hungry models and human-like flexibility. Neither humans nor machines reason from scratch; both operate by refining deeply embedded patterns in response to context. Although their mechanisms differ, the functional analogy remains instructive.

Understanding this layered architecture reframes the debate: intelligence is not a monolithic capacity, but a dynamic interplay between entrenched knowledge and context-sensitive adjustment. MACI's distinctive contribution is to preserve the generative efficiency of foundational LLMs while adding structured mechanisms: critique, role-switching, verification, and synthesis that elevate adaptation to the level of collective deliberation.

Understanding this layered architecture reframes the debate: intelligence is not a monolith, but a dynamic interplay between knowledge and contextual adaptation. MACI's contribution lies in preserving the generative efficiency of foundation models while adding structured mechanisms, including critique, role-switching, verification, and synthesis. These mechanisms collectively elevate adaptation to the level of collaborative reasoning.

Note: This aphorism establishes the foundational architectural insight behind MACI: intelligence arises from the interplay of a pretrained, data-driven substrate and a context-sensitive adaptive layer. It sets the stage for Aph. #5, where this adaptation layer becomes a programmable mechanism through contextual modulation, and for Aph. #8, which interprets this same layer as the functional analogue of consciousness, regulating behavior and intention. Together, these aphorisms define MACI's layered approach: preserving the efficiency of static models while enabling dynamic, deliberative reasoning through structured interaction.

Aph. #5: Context transforms capabilities

"Strength and weakness in an LLM are not fixed traits, but fluid, shifting with context. MACI enables models to transcend training biases and adopt new roles through structured interaction."

Language models are often evaluated in terms of static competencies. They are said to be "good" at summarization, "weak" at logical inference, or prone to certain biases. However, this evaluation misses a deeper principle: *LLM behavior is context-sensitive.* The same model can produce divergent results, depending on how it is prompted, instructed, or situated within a task.

This flexibility arises from the way LLMs generate responses. Without stable goals or persistent beliefs, they respond to cues embedded in context. Although this can lead to inconsistency or overfitting to recent tokens, it also allows *contextual modulation*, a process that alters behavior not through retraining but by shaping the context.

MACI turns this property into a core design principle. It treats context not as a constraint but as a *controllable layer of adaptation.* Through role assignment, dialogic structuring, and structured disagreement, MACI coordinates agents to respond differently than they would in isolation. In this sense, context becomes a functional *design surface*, which only directs behavior but configures the reasoning dynamics of the system itself.

Three principles illustrate this transformation:

1. *Bias is contextual.* A model that defaults to caution may suppress novel ideas in exploratory tasks but increase safety in medical settings. MACI manages these tradeoffs by assigning complementary roles and balancing behavior through interaction.

2. *Adaptation is interactional.* LLMs change tone, focus, and strategy when prompted to critique others, defend a viewpoint, or explore counterfactuals. MACI leverages these dynamics to increase the diversity of reasoning and improve convergence through dialogue.

3. *Capability is conditional.* Instead of retraining models for fixed competencies, MACI reuses the same model in multiple roles: analyst, skeptic, reconciler, each invoked by a distinct interaction pattern or instruction format. This modular role-switching reveals capacities that remain latent in static use.

These behavioral shifts are measurable. Prior work demonstrates that adjusting contentiousness levels, argumentative tone, and emphasis via role assignments directly influences the quality and diversity of reasoning [4]. Measures of information theory, such as mutual information and entropy reduction, quantify the transition from disagreement to consensus [6].

For example, in a medical triage task, two LLM agents can begin with divergent diagnoses: one emphasizes common symptoms, the other rare but high-risk causes. They engage in moderated debate across multiple rounds. As the dialogue progresses and context accumulates, each agent adapts. By the final round, they converge on a mutually defensible diagnosis that neither would have reached alone. This capability is not integrated into either model; it emerges from the way MACI configures the interaction.

This reframes the notion of "capability." It is no longer a fixed attribute of the model, but a *systemic outcome* shaped by contextual design. MACI assumes that intelligence emerges not from perfect individual models, but from how imperfect ones are placed into a structured, adaptive system.

Aphorism #5 builds on the structural insight of Aphorism #4 and draws its philosophical grounding from Aphorism #8. Both describe the two-layer model of intelligence: a foundation layer (the pretrained model) and an adaptation layer (external modulation through context, roles, or prompts). Here, the adaptation layer puts into action, not by altering internal weights but by shaping behavior through contextual control and agent coordination. What the model does depends not only on what it has learned, but on how the system chooses to engage it.

Note: This aphorism establishes contextual modulation as a central mechanism within MACI. It puts into action the adaptation layer introduced in Aphorism #4 and provides the functional foundation for Aph. #6 (linguistic role modulation), Aph. #7 (ethical alignment through institutional checks), and Aph. #10 (debate-driven refinement). These ideas are philosophically grounded in Aph. #8, which frames the adaptation layer as a regulatory analogue of consciousness: filtering the impulse into intention and shaping the outputs for public reasoning. Intelligence, in this light, is not fixed, but fluid, shaped by design, role, and interaction.

Aph. #6: Linguistic behavior reflects intention and emotions

"LLMs are designed and trained to emulate human linguistic endeavors, each aimed at fulfilling distinct human objectives."

Human language is rarely neutral; we speak and write with intention, to argue, explain, persuade, or connect. LLMs, trained on such purpose-driven language, inherit these communicative pat-

C.L.	Tone	Emphasis	Language
0.9	Most confrontational; raising strong ethical, scientific, and social objections.	Highlighting risks and downsides; ethical quandaries, unintended consequences, and exacerbation of inequalities.	Definitive and polarizing, e.g., "should NOT be allowed," "unacceptable risks," "inevitable disparities."
0.7	Still confrontational but open to some benefits, albeit overshadowed by negatives.	Acknowledging that some frameworks could make it safer or more equitable, while cautioning against its impl. challenges.	Less polarizing; "serious concerns remain," "needs more scrutiny."
0.5	Balanced; neither advocating strongly for nor against.	Equal weight on pros and cons; looking for a middle ground.	Neutral; "should be carefully considered," "both benefits and risks."
0.3	More agreeable than confrontational, with reservations.	Supportive but cautious; focus on ensuring ethical and equitable use.	Positive but careful; "impetus to ensure," "transformative potential."
0.0	Completely agreeable & supportive.	Focused on immense potential benefits; advocating for proactive adoption.	Very positive; "groundbreaking advance," "new era of possibilities."

Table 1.2: Linguistic features associated with varying contentiousness levels modeled by GPT-4

terns. Although they lack intrinsic emotions or beliefs, they can emulate the rhetorical strategies and discursive forms associated with specific roles.

Consider these role archetypes:

- *Journalist*: Presents coherent, factual narratives;
- *Debater*: Constructs and defends arguments;
- *Analyst*: Dissects problems and identifies patterns;
- *Mediator*: Synthesizes divergent viewpoints.

MACI assigns such roles deliberately, using structured prompts and interaction constraints to shape agent behavior. For example, in multi-agent debates, contentiousness is modeled by adjusting tone, emphasis, and word choice [4].

Beyond contentiousness, MACI also modulates emotional expression. Research [26] has shown that LLMs can be conditioned to generate outputs across affective spectrums, validated through both linguistic features and visual representations, as presented in Figure 1.1.

Figure 1.1: A lady and garden scene under different emotions. From top-left (happiest) to bottom-right (saddest).

This capacity to control linguistic behavior across both rhetorical and emotional dimensions allows MACI to orchestrate agent interactions in a goal-directed manner. The system uses language not only as output, but as a medium of coordination: assigning roles that reflect task demands and tuning the expressive style to support adaptive collaborative reasoning.

Aphorism #6 builds directly on Aphorism #5's principle of contextual modulation, showing that linguistic behavior is the primary mechanism through which MACI implements different roles and functions of the agent.

Note: Aphorism #6 builds on the principle of contextual modulation introduced in Aph. #5 by showing how linguistic behavior becomes the primary surface for adaptation. It provides the expressive substrate for enabling ethical alignment through role-based framing (Aph. #7). These behaviors are further synthesized in Aph. #10, where structured dialogue among diverse roles drives the quality of the reasoning. In MACI, language is not just the output: it is the interface of intention, strategy, and convergence.

Aph. #7: Checks and balances ensure adaptive alignment

"Separating knowledge discovery, ethical oversight, and behavioral evaluation into distinct roles ensures a system of checks and balances, promoting adaptable AI safety and alignment with cultural norms."

MACI implements a tripartite structure for adaptive alignment (Fig. 1.2), drawing inspiration from constitutional governance [7]:

- **Executive**: Generates knowledge, hypotheses, and solutions.
- **Legislative** (DIKE): Establishes ethical principles and constraints.
- **Judicial** (ERIS): Conducts a case-specific review and adversarial critique.

This separation avoids the pitfalls of reward-based fine-tuning approaches such as RLHF, which often conflate performance and ethics by directly altering model parameters. In contrast, MACI isolates knowledge production from value imposition. Ethical reasoning is externalized, not embedded in a static policy, enabling more transparent and interpretable adjustments.

Furthermore, by treating each instance independently through the judicial branch, MACI enables context-sensitive ethical alignment rather than applying averaged constraints that fail to account for individual situations and cultural or societal variations.

Moreover, by evaluating the alignment case by case through the judiciary branch, MACI adapts to the context and culture rather

Figure 1.2: Three Framework Components: Executive LLMs (bottom), Legislative (DIKE), and Judicial (ERIS).

than applying averaged constraints. A suitable solution in one setting can be flawed in another; MACI embraces this diversity by treating disagreement as a necessary mechanism for refinement, not failure.

Note: This aphorism builds on Aph. #5 (contextual modulation) and Aph. #6 (role-based linguistic behavior) by formalizing role separation for ethical alignment. It serves as a structural pillar for MACI's governance model, complementing Aph. #8, which frames intention regulation as a system-level control layer. Together, these mechanisms support Aph. #10's collaborative reasoning and Aph. #11's dissipation of hallucination through adversarial validation. In MACI, alignment is not imposed; it is deliberated.

Aph. #8: Consciousness filters impulse; MACI governs LLMs

"Our public behavior is not a direct, unfiltered output from our unconscious mind. Instead, consciousness regulates and refines the underlying impulses, ensuring that our actions are aligned with social norms. Similarly, MACI *frameworks harness and temper the inherent tendencies of LLMs, mitigating inherited biases."*

Philosophers and psychologists describe consciousness as a regulatory system that filters impulsive or inappropriate actions before they reach the public sphere. Freud characterizes the ego as a mediator that suppresses and channels the raw desires of the id [27]. Kant views reason as a regulator of inclination, aligning behavior with duty and rational constraints [28]. Sartre argues that consciousness introduces delay and reflection, inserting "nothingness" between stimulus and action [29]. Across these views, consciousness acts as a gatekeeper, transforming a raw impulse into socially and ethically acceptable behavior.

MACI performs an analogous function. Although it does not implement consciousness, it regulates the outputs of LLMs using contextual, structural, and ethical constraints. Neuroscientific models such as Gazzaniga's "interpreter" theory [30] and Baars' Global Workspace Theory [31] also frame consciousness as an aggregator and filter of lower-level cognitive processes. In line with these ideas, MACI applies higher-order control mechanisms to shape model behavior through:

- *Inhibitory control:* Suppressing harmful, incoherent, or inappropriate content;
- *Reappraisal:* Reframing outputs based on ethical, epistemic, or pragmatic considerations;

- *Contextualization:* Adjusting tone, abstraction, and intent based on task demands and audience.

This architecture reflects the functionalist modeling approach presented in our CoCoMo work [3]. CoCoMo treats consciousness not as awareness or qualia, but as an executive control system that coordinates modular reasoning. MACI adopts this perspective explicitly: intention regulation governs when and how LLMs generate language suitable for deliberation, decision-making, and social exchange.

Note: This aphorism establishes the **regulatory foundation** of MACI, drawing from philosophical, neuroscientific, and architectural perspectives on cognitive control. Like consciousness, MACI inserts deliberation between thought and action, ensuring that outputs reflect structured goals rather than impulsive inference. It provides the conceptual basis for Aphorism #5 (contextual control), Aph. #6 (behavioral modulation), and Aph. #7 (ethical alignment through institutional checks); and it prepares the ground for collaborative refinement through interaction, debate, and convergence in Aphorisms #9–11. Intelligence, in this view, is not measured solely by what it produces, but by how it governs what it allows to emerge.

Aph. #9: The essence of precise questioning

"The essence lies in framing and sequencing the right questions."

This aphorism underscores the foundational role of precise questioning in multi-agent LLM systems. The approach draws on the Socratic tradition, where knowledge does not arise from assertion but from systematic inquiry [32]. Within MACI, particularly

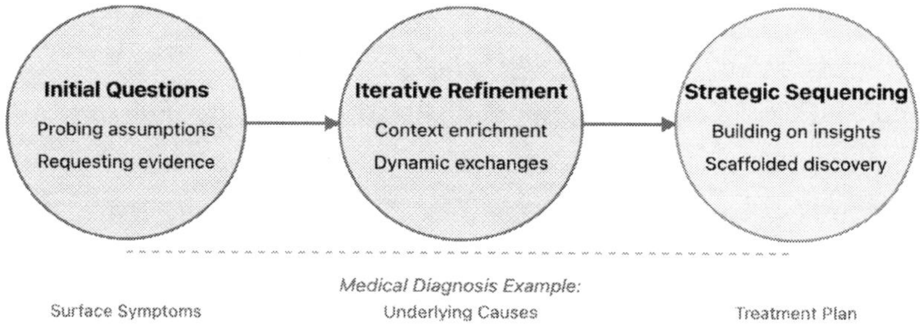

Figure 1.3: LLM Question Progression Framework.

through the SocraSynth framework [4], three key principles structure this process:

First, the quality of multi-LLM dialogue hinges on how effectively agents interrogate one another. Strong counterarguments function as probing questions: they surface hidden assumptions, demand justification, and expose logical tension. In this sense, the Socratic elenchus becomes a dialogic protocol: not to defeat, but to discover.

Second, iterative exchanges sharpen intent over time. Early questions may be exploratory, even vague, but as context accumulates, agents refine their inquiries with increasing precision. Each response becomes a scaffold for the next query, creating a feedback loop of progressive clarification.

Third, beyond formulation, the sequencing of questions becomes crucial. Ordering determines the scope and relevance of subsequent investigation. In MACI, agents use prior turns to dynamically plan next-step inquiries, allowing structured traversal across complex domains. This logic mirrors hypothesis refinement in scientific inquiry, starting with exploratory breadth and then narrowing through informed follow-up.

This virtuous cycle—precise questioning, contextual enrichment, and adaptive sequencing—drives the depth and utility of MACI's reasoning. For example, in medical classification, a discussion that begins with the enumeration of symptoms can evolve into causal analysis, exploration of comorbidities, and synthesis of treatments [6, 33]. Here, a human moderator adjusts the agents' linguistic stances, from contentious to conciliatory, using information-theoretic signals such as cross-entropy, mutual information, and Jensen-Shannon divergence to optimize epistemic progress.

This virtuous cycle of precise questioning, contextual enrichment, and strategic sequencing determines the quality and utility of the insights generated by LLMs.

Example: A conversation that begins with a question about the symptoms of a disease can evolve into a diagnostic discussion as LLMs build on each other's insights. The discussion transitions from identifying surface-level symptoms to uncovering underlying causes, recognizing comorbidities, and generating actionable treatment recommendations [6, 33]. To facilitate effective sequencing, moving from exploration of possible diseases to deeper probing of finalists, the conversation moderator adjusts the LLMs' linguistic behaviors, shifting from contentious to conciliatory tones based on several information-theory metrics, including cross-entropy, mutual information, and Jensen-Shannon divergence.

Note: Aphorism #9 serves as a cognitive engine for the MACI framework. It underpins Aphorism #6 by guiding how linguistic roles shape intention, and supports Aphorism #10 by structuring debate through layered, clarifying inquiry. It enables Aphorism #11 by progressively narrowing the hallucination space, and lays the groundwork for Aphorisms #12 and #13 by prompting the kinds of questions that foster cross-domain synthesis and emergent learning. Well-sequenced questioning, in this light, becomes the

Figure 1.4: The MACI Framework with Two Socrates.

scaffolding for adaptive reasoning across the system.

In short, precise questioning is not just a technique; it is the substrate for coordination, divergence, synthesis, and convergence in the collaborative intelligence of MACI. It determines what becomes knowable.

Aph. #10: Debate strengthens reasoning quality

"Critical thinking requires more than one Socrates."

The power of collaborative reasoning has deep philosophical roots. While Socrates transformed thinking through systematic questioning, even he recognized the necessity of dialogue partners. As Aristotle formalizes, dialectic requires both thesis and antithesis to approach synthesis [34]. This principle finds one of its most profound expressions in Hegel's dialectical process, where knowledge advances not through linear accumulation but through the *productive tension* (SocraSynth's "contentiousness" [4]) of opposing ideas [12]. In Hegel's framework, an initial position (thesis) confronts its negation (antithesis), producing a higher-order understanding (synthesis) that transcends yet preserves both. This dialectical movement mirrors how MACI orchestrates productive disagreement to generate deeper insight.

First, in dialectical reasoning, each LLM serves both as a questioner and as a respondent. Like Socrates engaging with interlocutors, one LLM challenges assumptions while another defends or refines them. This dynamic creates what philosopher Hannah Arendt calls the "in-between space," where meaning emerges from the interaction itself [35]. Each exchange builds upon prior reasoning, refining hypotheses through mutual scrutiny. This process exemplifies Hegel's concept of *Aufhebung* (sublation), where opposing viewpoints are not only compromised but transformed into a qualitatively new understanding.

Second, meaningful collaboration requires a *baseline* level of competency. Just as Socrates could not derive insight from those lacking reasoning capacity, MACI cannot produce valuable outcomes when the participating models are fundamentally weak. Two poor reasoners do not combine into one strong one; their limitations may compound rather than cancel out. Fortunately, with the rise of advanced LLMs, we have crossed a critical competency threshold, enabling collaborative reasoning that can identify and correct individual model limitations. Moreover, as Aph. #11 demonstrates, hallucinations tend to dissipate in a well-orchestrated multi-LLM dialogue, reinforcing the value of structured collaboration.

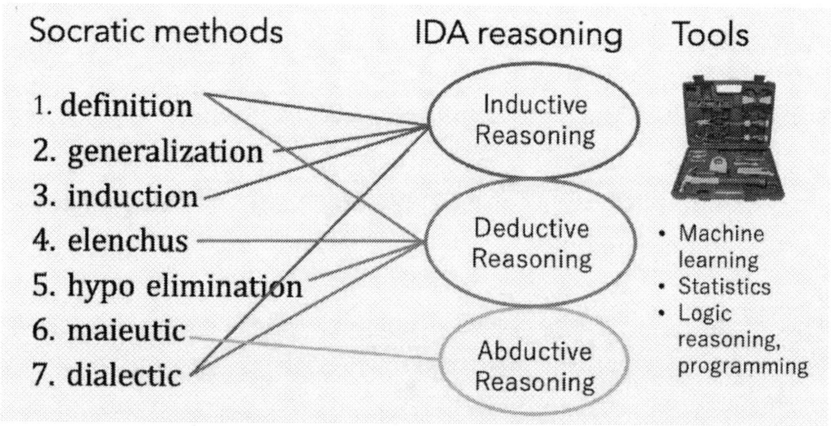

Figure 1.5: CRIT: Critical Inquisitive Template. Mapping from individual Socratic methods to reasoning methods.

Third, the depth of dialogue varies with the sophistication of the participants. Advanced LLMs (e.g., Claude 3.7, GPT-4o, and DeepSeek R1) can explore complex ideas in depth, leveraging diverse training and reasoning strategies to interrogate and challenge each other's assumptions. In contrast, smaller models produce only shallow exchanges, like novices grappling with philosophical questions they cannot fully articulate. Model diversity, in training data, architectural assumptions, and epistemic behavior, becomes a necessary condition for productive debate.

MACI creates a space for *AI philosophers* to engage in structured dialogue through systems such as SocraSynth and DIKE-ERIS, with EVINCE monitoring information flow and CRIT [5] evaluating the quality of reasoning. The strength of these debates depends not only on the frameworks themselves but on the capabilities and calibration of the participants. This understanding guides both model selection and the realistic expectations we place on their collaborative outputs.

This approach suggests that the path to artificial general intelligence may not lie in scaling individual models alone, but in orchestrating systems of capable, diverse agents engaged in structured debate, mirroring how human insight often emerges socially. As Karl Jaspers observed, "Truth begins between people" [36], a principle that appears equally applicable to artificial minds seeking mutual understanding.

Note: This aphorism connects with Aph. #1 (truth as perspectival synthesis), Aph. #9 (the role of precise questioning), and Aph. #11 (hallucination reduction through orchestration). Together, they illuminate how MACI turns disagreement into a productive engine of reasoning: where structured dialogue refines claims, filters errors, and advances collective understanding beyond the capacity of any single agent.

Aph. #11: Hallucinations fade under scrutiny

"Hallucinations rarely repeat."

Have you ever wondered why recurring nightmares, though similar in theme, never unfold in exactly the same way? This property of human dreaming finds a parallel in the behavior of LLM hallucinations, which also resist exact repetition, even when the prompt remains unchanged.

This observation echoes long-standing insights from psychology and philosophy. Freud noted that unconscious repetition occurs not through identical images, but through symbolic variation and displacement [37]. Clinical studies of hallucinations in schizophrenia and substance use disorders similarly reveal that while themes may recur, verbal or visual content almost always changes with each episode [38]. Phenomenologists such as Merleau-Ponty argued that perception is never static: Each encounter is shaped by shifting contextual salience and embodied interpretation [39].

This phenomenon also applies to LLMs. Hallucinations arise when the probabilistic token prediction generates unstable or unsupported sequences from ambiguous inputs. Because outputs are sampled from a probability distribution, similar prompts can produce different hallucinations. This distinguishes hallucinations from systematic errors, which recur due to model bias or data gaps.

In MACI frameworks such as SocraSynth [4, 6], this non-repetitive nature becomes an asset. When one agent produces a hallucination, others can challenge it. As dialogue evolves, the shared context becomes increasingly specific, constraining the "hallucination space." With each round, it becomes harder for the original agent to restate the same fabrication; instead, it must align with grounded knowledge or admit uncertainty. Through structured disagreement, hallucinations naturally dissipate.

In addition, hallucinations are sporadic, while true knowledge gaps are consistent. To distinguish the two, MACI integrates Retrieval-Augmented Generation (RAG), enabling access to verifiable sources. This allows the system to triage stochastic noise versus persistent ignorance and apply targeted remediation.

Example: In a multi-agent dialogue about historical events, LLM_A might initially hallucinate that "The Treaty of Versailles was signed in 1921." LLM_B challenges this: "The Treaty of Versailles was signed in 1919, following World War I." On a second query, LLM_A is unlikely to repeat the same error—now grounded by the updated context. Even if it errs again, the mistake is likely to differ in form, making it detectable through further rounds of scrutiny [40].

This understanding has implications for system design: hallucinations are not persistent constructs but unstable artifacts of uncertain inference. Rather than requiring static classifiers, MACI uses multi-agent dialogue to destabilize hallucinations through context evolution. What vanishes under scrutiny is not just the false claim, but its power to recur.

Note: This aphorism complements Aph. #10 (Debate strengthens reasoning quality) and Aph. #2 (External mirrors enable validation). It shows that hallucinations fade not because they are explicitly detected, but because structured dialogue progressively eliminates unsupported claims. MACI transforms stochastic unreliability into epistemic refinement: hallucination becomes not a flaw but a transient signal that dissolves in the presence of discourse.

Aph. #12: Polydisciplinary synthesis forges new frontiers

"LLMs are not taught about domain boundaries, as they were trained only to predict the next words. This polydisciplinary approach to information representation allows LLMs to synthesize knowledge that might be beyond narrowly focused, domain-specific human understanding."

The term *polydisciplinary* was introduced by Microsoft's Chief Scientific Officer, Eric Horvitz, during a Stanford HAI symposium in 2023. He observed that GPT-4, trained via maximum likelihood estimation, applies the same statistical machinery whether processing quantum physics or Shakespearean sonnets: the model learns without internalizing disciplinary boundaries.

Although humans organize knowledge into categories such as physics, poetry, biology, and philosophy, LLMs move fluidly across these divisions, unaware of traditional boundaries. This polydisciplinary capacity opens new possibilities [41] (Chapter 14):

- When an LLM perceives a pattern linking Shakespearean verse and quantum mechanics, it does not question whether such a connection is conceptually permissible.
- Complex problems that traditionally require interdisciplinary expertise become accessible to LLMs, which operate freely beyond academic silos.
- Novel hypotheses may emerge precisely because LLMs do not filter out connections conventionally deemed implausible or inappropriate by domain norms.

This boundary-free synthesis mirrors what cognitive scientists Gilles Fauconnier and Mark Turner call *conceptual blending*, a process by which novel insights emerge from the fusion of distinct conceptual spaces [42]. When asked to relate music theory to protein folding, an LLM proposed modeling protein sequences as melodies, enabling motif-based visualizations. When comparing architecture and immunology, it described the immune system as a "defensive architecture," inspiring layered design analogies for system resilience. These examples illustrate how LLMs emulate the core structure of human creativity: not by refining within a single domain but by blending conceptual frameworks across them.

MACI harnesses this capability through frameworks such as SocraSynth [4], EVINCE [6], and the DIKE–ERIS dual model [7]. Together, these tools help formulate meaningful questions (Aph. #9), synthesize novel perspectives (Aph. #10), and filter out incoherence (Aph. #11). The result is a system that not only traverses known fields, but probes the "unknown unknowns" with epistemic discipline.

The essence of MACI lies in enabling humans and LLMs to co-navigate the liminal spaces between disciplines, those intellectually rich but cognitively uncertain zones where novel concepts are born. In these moments, humans serve not as oracles but as moderators, evaluating, anchoring, and refining what emerges from polydisciplinary synthesis.

The essence of MACI lies in the navigation of interdisciplinary intersections, areas where genuine insight often emerges. These liminal spaces, naturally traversed by LLMs, are rich in potential but saturated with ambiguity: the domain of "unknown unknowns." Humans may struggle to pose coherent questions or distinguish signal from noise in such terrain. In these cases, MACI encourages minimal human interference. Rather than steering the process, humans act as lightweight moderators, providing initial prompts, then stepping back to let the system explore freely and critically assess its own findings. This arrangement allows MACI to illuminate uncharted intellectual territory with autonomy, surfacing connections, and hypotheses that extend beyond conventional human foresight. Chapter 14 [41] offers an example that spans several unexpected knowledge domains, seeded by a single biblical narrative.

This capacity for polydisciplinary synthesis represents perhaps the most promising path toward artificial general intelligence (AGI) and beyond. True innovation requires the ability to forge new frontiers by perceiving novel connections across traditional boundaries, to see patterns invisible to specialists entrenched in disciplinary silos. Human innovation often requires rare interdisciplinary genius, and LLMs inherently operate beyond these constraints, potentially discovering insights and opening intellectual frontiers that might otherwise remain unexplored for decades. In this sense, the polydisciplinary nature of LLMs does not just enhance existing knowledge; it creates the conditions for genuine intellectual exploration into uncharted territories.

Note: This aphorism builds on the adaptive structures in Aph. #5 and the intention-regulatory framing of Aph. #8. It provides the epistemic ground for Aph. #9 (question formulation) and the generative substrate for Aph. #10–11 (collaborative refinement). Polydisciplinary synthesis is not noise; it is a structured divergence that expands the frontier of *knowability*.

Aph. #13: Human heuristics are limited and end-to-end learning shows supremacy

"When machines are freed from handcrafted features and human biases, they often surpass what even expert-designed systems can achieve."

Across several landmark domains in AI, a recurring pattern has emerged: systems trained end-to-end, mapping raw inputs directly to outputs, often outperform those built with hand-crafted heuristics or modular pipelines. These breakthroughs illustrate the limitations of human-designed rules and the power of self-learned representations given sufficient data, compute, and architecture.

Consider AlphaGo versus AlphaGo Zero. The original AlphaGo, which defeated world champion Lee Sedol in 2016, relied on expert games and human-derived features [43]. AlphaGo Zero, in contrast, was learned solely from self-play via reinforcement learning. Within days, it surpasses its predecessor, revealing that human priors can restrict learning in expressive models [44].

A similar transition occurred in protein folding. AlphaFold v1 used co-evolutionary heuristics; AlphaFold 2 employed a fully differentiable architecture, predicting 3D structure directly from amino acid sequences. It won CASP14 by a wide margin [45], showcasing how task-specific structure can emerge from data alone.

In autonomous driving, earlier systems were modular, perception, prediction, planning, each engineered separately. But these pipelines suffered from cascading errors and brittleness in the edge case. Newer systems such as Tesla's end-to-end stack or Wayve's policy networks map directly from raw vision to actions, enabling more robust generalization [46, 47].

In computer vision, SIFT was once the gold standard for handcrafted geometric features [48]. Then came AlexNet, a deep convolutional network trained directly on pixels. Its performance on ImageNet rendered the heuristic approach obsolete almost overnight [49]. More than accuracy, the shift was about *adaptivity*: data-driven models [50, 51, 52] can improve through feedback; fixed pipelines cannot.

These examples converge on a central insight: human intuition, while useful for bootstrapping progress, imposes biases and boundaries. End-to-end learning removes these constraints, allowing models to learn optimal representations jointly across all layers of reasoning.

MACI embraces this insight in its reasoning framework. Although human rules shape safety and ethical constraints (see Aph. #7), robust understanding arises when agents learn reasoning (Aph. #1, #10), critique, and reflection through interaction. Frameworks such as CRIT [5] operationalize this: instead of coding decision rules, CRIT prompts agents to evaluate each other's claims, sourcing credibility and logical strength from collective deliberation.

Just as organisms evolve not through static rule books but through continuous adaptation [24, 53], intelligence in machines emerges not from rigid design but from learning by feedback [54]. End-to-end systems outperform not because they ignore structure, but because they build structure in service of adaptation.

Note: This aphorism complements Aph. #12, where polydisciplinary synthesis emerges from LLMs' boundary-free representations. Here, we see that eliminating rigid heuristics—whether domain-specific or architectural—frees learning to discover new forms of generalization. Together, these aphorisms argue for a model of intelligence rooted not in static human priors, but in fluid, adaptive exploration across conceptual, structural, and epistemic boundaries.

Aph. #14: AGI emerges through collaborative intelligence

"The path to AGI lies not in singular models, but in systems that reflect, regulate, and reason together."

Artificial general intelligence will not arise by merely scaling language models [55], nor by perfecting a monolithic architecture. Instead, it will emerge from *systems of collaboration* architectures in which multiple agents operate with distinct roles, epistemic lenses, and regulatory feedback loops. These systems must do more than generate fluent responses: they must interrogate their own reasoning, revise their conclusions, and reconcile divergent viewpoints in pursuit of coherence and truth.

Recent evidence from OpenAI's 4o1 experiments shows that inference-time scaling, allocating tokens for deliberation or chain-of-thought, improves reasoning and planning performance with only linear cost increases. Table 1.3 contrasts the tradeoffs between training-time and inference-time scaling, suggesting that dynamic, task-specific reasoning may be more fruitful than ever-larger training runs.

Dimension	Training Scaling	Inference Scaling
Cost scaling	Exponential / Superlinear	Linear (per output token)
Accuracy gain	Diminishing returns (esp. at scale)	High marginal gains on hard tasks
Flexibility	Fixed post-training	Adaptive (per input/task)
Model size	Must grow for gains	Fixed model
Alignment to reasoning	Limited	High (via thinking tokens, CoT, debate)

Table 1.3: Comparison of Training Scaling vs. Inference Scaling in LLM Performance

This shift in perspective is central to MACI. In SocraSynth and EVINCE, agents pursue truth through Socratic dialogue. In CRIT, claims are evaluated for coherence and evidentiary strength. In DIKE–ERIS, moral and cultural norms are enforced via institutional-style checks. SagaLLM enables long-horizon planning by providing persistent memory, constraint validation, and workflow guarantees.

Yet such systems cannot function without a planner. Enter ALAS (Adaptive Layered Agent System), which orchestrates distributed planning and role assignment. Where SagaLLM ensures consistency, ALAS decomposes tasks, manages dependencies, and coordinates execution between agents operating in real-world domains such as ride-sharing, logistics, or collaborative robotics, domains where static LLM reasoning often fails.

These subsystems embody a larger truth: *no single model can model itself*, just as no mind can achieve objectivity without encountering other minds.

Where Aphorism #2 emphasized the need for external mirrors to validate outputs, Aphorism #14 transforms that insight into a design philosophy. MACI is not just a critique; it is a blueprint: *modularity, reflectivity, and role specialization* as the pillars of general intelligence. This architecture suggests that AGI will not emerge from raw scale, but from systems that are *aware of their own fallibility* and structured to adapt through principled dialogue.

This view responds to foundational critiques (e.g., LeCun's), which cite LLMs' lack of grounding, memory, and planning. We agree if one expects these to emerge from a single architecture. But we instead treat LLMs as a linguistic substrate, an artificial unconscious. Although they lack volition, they provide the generative and semantic flexibility upon which memory, control, and reasoning layers can be built.

Just as human intelligence arises not in isolation but through community, language, and institutional learning, **artificial general intelligence may arise not from singular mastery, but from collaborative coherence**.

The fourteen aphorisms unfold in a layered progression that mirrors the architecture of MACI itself. Aphorisms #1–#4 establish the philosophical foundation: they frame truth as perspectival, highlight the necessity of external validation, and introduce a layered view of intelligence that blends simulation with structured reasoning. These insights motivate the architectural strategies developed in Aphorisms #5–#8, where contextual modulation, role-based behavior, and institutional checks define how LLMs are coordinated, constrained, and guided within collaborative systems.

Aphorisms #9–#12 then describe how intelligence operates within this framework: through strategic questioning, dialectical engagement, hallucination mitigation, and polydisciplinary synthesis. This middle stratum reflects the operational core of MACI, where the reasoning is not housed in individual agents, but arises through structured interaction.

Finally, Aphorisms #13 and #14 widen the lens. They reject the notion that AGI will emerge solely through scale, and instead propose that general intelligence arises through modular cooperation, reflective regulation, and distributed coherence. Together, these aphorisms form more than a sequence—they constitute a system, where each conceptual layer scaffolds the next. From epistemic humility to architectural design and from behavioral control to intelligent emergence, they chart a coherent path toward collaborative artificial general intelligence.

Aphorism Theme Summary To illuminate the conceptual architecture of the MACI framework, Table 1.4 organizes the fourteen aphorisms by thematic pillars. Each theme captures a core dimension of collaborative intelligence, ranging from epistemological foundations and behavioral simulation to cognitive regulation, ethical governance, and the synthesis required for AGI. Several aphorisms appear under multiple themes, reflecting their integrative nature. This organization provides a high-level map of how the components of MACI interact, align, and build toward a unified system of multi-agent reasoning and adaptive intelligence.

Epistemology and Perspective
#1. Truth through perspectives
#2. External validation
#9. Precise questioning
#10. Dialectical debate
#12. Polydisciplinary synthesis
Simulation and Role Enactment
#3. Simulated reasoning
#5. Contextual modulation
#6. Linguistic behavior
#13. End-to-end learning
Cognitive Architecture and Control
#4. Foundation and adaptation
#5. Contextual modulation
#8. Intention regulation
#13. End-to-end learning
Governance, Ethics, and Alignment
#2. External validation
#7. Checks and balances
#8. Intention regulation
#11. Hallucination dissipation
Synthesis Toward AGI
#10. Dialectical debate
#12. Polydisciplinary synthesis
#13. End-to-end learning
#14. Collaborative AGI

Table 1.4: Aphorisms Grouped by Thematic Pillars in MACI. An aphorism may be listed under multiple pillars.

2 A Brief History of AI: From Turing to Transformers

Abstract This chapter reinterprets the history of AI, focusing on the evolution of similarity measurement, from rule-based to context-aware models, and emphasizing its critical role in AI's core functions like learning and problem-solving. It explores the impact of detailed and evolving understandings of similarity in linguistics (text) and computer vision (image), projecting a future where AI merges advanced data analysis with abstract reasoning. The chapter will provide an in-depth analysis from the perspectives of linguistics, computer science, and cognitive psychology/neuroscience, illustrating how the progression of similarity concepts continues to fuel AI's advancement.

Introduction

Artificial Intelligence (AI) has journeyed through a fascinating historical trajectory, marked by five pivotal epochs that each represent significant paradigm shifts triggered by major technological advancements. The epochs are as follows: *Initiation*, setting the stage with foundational concepts and milestones of AI; *Expert System Encoding Human Knowledge*, where AI systems were predominantly rule-based, encoding and applying human expertise; *Heuristic-Based Modeling*, which highlights the era of developing and using heuristic methods for AI problem-solving; *Learning Model from Data*, focusing on the transition to algorithms that learn and adapt from data, signifying the emergence of machine learning; and *Context-Based Semantic Disambiguation*, highlighting AI's evolving proficiency in understanding and interpreting context, thereby improving semantic accuracy.

While numerous comprehensive sources, such as Wikipedia, provide detailed accounts of AI's evolution through various lenses: language, computation, philosophy, cognitive psychology, neuroscience, and application–this chapter takes a different path. It zeroes in on a fundamental aspect: **similarity**.

When we consider the intelligence of machines, we often focus on attributes such as learning capacity, pattern recognition, predictive accuracy, robustness, adaptability, generalization, reasoning, problem-solving, and decision making abilities. These qualities collectively define the prowess of AI systems. Among these traits, the concept of similarity plays a pivotal role. For instance, in learning, an effective similarity measure is fundamental for recognizing patterns and generalizing knowledge. In terms of adaptability, the ability to detect similarities to previous experiences allows AI to adjust to new or evolving circumstances. Regarding robustness, employing similarity measures helps AI differentiate between normal and anomalous patterns, thereby increasing its resilience. Furthermore, in the realm of problem-solving, the capacity to identify similarities to previously encountered situations can enable AI to apply existing solutions to new problems, enhancing its efficacy in addressing challenges. This chapter explores the vital function of similarity across the broad spectrum of AI capabilities, underlining its significant contribution to the field's foundational operations.

In the realm of tangible objects, similarity measures are integral to various vision-related tasks, aiding in the recognition of patterns, shapes, and colors, which are essential for object recognition and image classification. In text analysis, these measures are crucial for identifying similarities in content, aiding in plagiarism detection, document retrieval, and language translation. In the auditory domain, similarity analysis of sound wave patterns or musical notes is key to genre classification and music recommendation systems. In medical imagery, these measures facilitate disease diagnosis by comparing patient images with known cases, enabling accurate medical condition identification and classification. Object feature comparison is foundational in robotics and surveillance for recognizing and interacting with physical entities. Similarly, facial and voice recognition systems rely on analyzing patterns to identify or verify identities, enhancing security and personal authentication. In e-commerce, similarity in product attributes or user preferences informs recommendation systems, enhancing user experience by suggesting related or complementary products.

In the abstract realm, similarity measures are crucial for discerning semantic relationships, aiding in knowledge representation, ontology mapping, and refining AI's interpretive faculties. Environmental studies leverage these assessments for climate modeling and ecological research. Sentiment analysis in social media or customer feedback utilizes similarity to extract insights into public sentiment or consumer behavior. These measures also underpin AI's problem-solving prowess in complex scenarios, informing strategy formulation. Behavioral analysis, whether in psychology or marketing, employs similarity comparisons to decode human actions and preferences. In the legal field, case similarity aids in judicial decision-making and legal scholarship. Language translation harnesses similarity in linguistic structures to break down language barriers. Furthermore, in creative writing, analyzing thematic or stylistic similarities assists in authorship identification, genre categorization, and literary exploration.

The advancement in similarity research, while appearing gradual, reflects not only human ingenuity but also the limitations imposed by computational resources and hardware capabilities. The quest to quantify similarity covers a broad spectrum of abstractions, from sensory inputs like visual, auditory, olfactory, and tactile data to complex abstract concepts such as ideas and semantics. Hardware improvements have enabled researchers to explore more advanced methods that encompass both concrete and abstract forms of similarity. This progression marks the field's growth in harmonizing detailed sensory data analysis with a deeper understanding of abstract concepts, utilizing computational advancements and diverse data interpretations.

Following sections will provide a deeper dive into key AI terminology and the development of similarity measures in two distinctive views: scientific disciplines and historical evolution. The disciplinary view encompasses three key perspectives: linguistics, computer science, cognitive psychology, and neuroscience. The evolution view traces the historical journey of similarity measurement through distinct eras: rule-based, model-based, data-centric, and context-aware.

Providing two views on similarity measurements–across different scientific disciplines and through the historical evolution of AI methodologies–offers a comprehensive understanding that caters to a broader audience with varied interests and backgrounds. Here are some reasons why this dual perspective is valuable:

Multidisciplinary Insight: Examining similarity measurements from different scientific disciplines enriches the understanding by high-

lighting how various fields approach and apply the concept of similarity. This can foster interdisciplinary collaboration and innovation, as techniques from one field can inspire new approaches in another.
Historical Context: Exploring how similarity measurement has evolved within AI provides historical context, showcasing how methodologies have progressed from rule-based to more advanced context-aware systems. This perspective helps readers appreciate the advancements in AI and understand why certain methods were developed or abandoned.

2.1 Definitions

We define and scope key terms and concepts to prepare for subsequent discussion.

2.1.1 Rudimentary Terms

Data: The raw information used to train AI models. Data quality significantly impacts model performance.
Algorithm: A set of instructions that a computer follows to perform a specific task. AI algorithms are often complex and involve statistical methods.
Model: A representation of the learned knowledge from data that allows the AI system to make predictions or decisions.

2.1.2 General Terms

Artificial Intelligence (AI): The broader concept of machines being able to carry out tasks in a way that we would consider smart.
Explainable AI: AI systems that offer transparency and an understanding of their operations and decision-making processes.

General AI: General AI, also known as Artificial General Intelligence (AGI), refers to a type of AI that has the ability to understand, learn, and apply knowledge in a wide range of tasks, much like a human being. It's an AI system with generalized human cognitive abilities, meaning that when presented with an unfamiliar task, it can find a solution without human intervention. AGI would be able to reason, solve problems, make judgments, plan, learn, and communicate in natural language, among other capabilities. However, as of now, AGI remains a theoretical concept and has not been realized in practical applications.

Narrow AI: Narrow AI, in contrast, is the type of AI that we encounter in our daily lives and is currently in use around the world. It is designed to perform a narrow task (e.g., facial recognition, internet searches, driving a car) and is trained for a specific dataset or a set of tasks. Narrow AI operates under a limited pre-defined range or context, often focusing on executing a single task extremely well or carrying out a limited range of tasks in a specific domain. It lacks the general cognitive abilities of AGI and cannot apply its knowledge beyond its specific field or task.

Machine Learning (ML): A subset of AI that includes statistical techniques that enable machines to improve at tasks with experience.

Deep Learning: A subset of machine learning that uses neural networks with three or more layers. These neural networks attempt to simulate the behavior of the human brain–albeit far from matching its ability–allowing it to "learn" from large amounts of data.

Neural Networks Computational models that are somewhat inspired by the structure of the human brain, enabling computers to recognize patterns and solve common problems in AI, such as classification, prediction, and decision making.

Supervised Learning: A type of machine learning where the model is provided with labeled training data and the desired output. The goal is to learn a mapping from inputs to outputs.

Unsupervised Learning: A type of machine learning where the model is not provided with labeled data and must find structure in its input on its own.

Reinforcement Learning: An area of machine learning where an agent learns to behave in an environment by performing actions and seeing the results, focusing on long-term rewards. An example is an AI agent learning to play a game through trial and error, receiving rewards for winning.

Natural Language Processing (NLP): A field of AI that gives machines the ability to read, understand, and derive meaning from human languages.

Computer Vision: A field of AI that trains computers to interpret and understand the visual world, extracting information from images and videos.

Robotics: The branch of technology that deals with the design, construction, operation, and application of robots, often incorporating AI systems to enhance autonomy and adaptability.

Large Language Model (LLM):. LLMs are advanced artificial intelligence systems trained on extensive datasets, initially text-centric and now increasingly incorporating multimodal data. They are designed to comprehend, generate, and interact with human language, imagery, and video with a level of sophistication that closely mirrors human cognitive processes.

2.1.3 Performance Terms

Algorithmic Bias: Algorithmic bias refers to the potential for algorithms to reflect, perpetuate, or amplify biases present in the training data or as a result of the design of the algorithms themselves. This can lead to skewed or unfair outcomes, particularly in decision-making processes.

Hallucination: In the context of AI, hallucination refers to the phenomenon where a model generates or outputs information that is ungrounded, misleading, or not supported by the input data. This is commonly seen in language models where the generated text may be plausible but not factually accurate or relevant to the context.

Generalization: Generalization is the ability of an AI model to perform well on new, unseen data that was not part of the training set. It indicates the model's capacity to apply learned knowledge to different situations, a key indicator of its robustness and utility.

Overfitting: Overfitting occurs when an AI model learns the details and noise in the training data to the extent that it negatively impacts the model's performance on new data. This usually happens when the model is too complex, capturing patterns that do not generalize to unseen data.

2.2 Perspectives on Similarity

This section presents the foundational theories of similarity measurement from three distinct domains: *linguistics*, *computer science*, and *cognitive psychology & neuroscience*. The upcoming historical section will clarify how these foundational theories have influenced and been incorporated into specific technological advancements and methodologies across various eras. Cross-references will be provided to ensure coherence and to emphasize the interconnection of these perspectives.

2.2.1 Linguistic Perspective

The study of similarity within linguistics has been profoundly influenced by Zellig Harris's pioneering work. His 1954 study introduced the idea that the distributional properties of words and their contextual usage could unlock the secrets of language comprehension, highlighting the indispensable role of context [56]. This principle, that words found in similar contexts tend to share meanings, laid the foundation for distributional semantics and resonates with John R. Firth's insight that "A word is known by the company it keeps." This linguistic perspective sets the stage for further exploration of how context and distributional properties have been instrumental in shaping our understanding of semantic similarity, paving the way for subsequent advancements in the field.

The evolution of linguistic theories continued into the latter part of the 20th century with the rise of cognitive linguistics, which examines the interplay between linguistic structures and human cognitive processes. This approach underscored how language reflects our perception and conceptualization of the world, introducing a multi-layered perspective on semantic abstraction.

A significant milestone in bridging linguistic theory with practical applications was the development of WordNet in the 1980s by a team at Princeton University [57]. This lexical database, which organizes English words into sets of cognitive synonyms or *synsets*, has profoundly influenced areas such as word sense disambiguation, information retrieval, and beyond, highlighting the importance of structured semantic relationships in understanding language.

Moreover, the influence of linguistic insights extended into the domain of computer vision with the creation of ImageNet by Fei-Fei Li [58], which drew upon the principles underlying WordNet to categorize visual content. This convergence of linguistics and computer science has been further propelled by advancements in computational methods, with techniques like Latent Semantic Analysis (LSA) [59], Latent Dirichlet Allocation (LDA) [60], and innovative word embeddings such as Word2Vec [61] and GloVe [62]. These methodologies have enabled the conceptualization of word meanings in high-dimensional spaces, illuminating the intricate web of semantic relationships through patterns of co-occurrence and contextual analysis.

The introduction of the transformer model [63] and the subsequent unveiling of BERT [64], which employs self-supervised learning to predict masked words within a context, along with the release of GPT, designed to predict the next word based on context, heralded a new epoch in our endeavor to unravel context-dependent semantics. This development fulfills the vision proposed by Zellig Harris in his groundbreaking 1954 work, now actualized in contemporary computational models.

2.2.2 Computer Science Perspective

In computer science, the concept of similarity has evolved from simple rule-based models to complex vector-space and probabilistic models, reflecting the field's progression in addressing various computational challenges.

A. Rule-Based

A rule-based AI model, also known as an expert system, employs a collection of predefined if-then statements to execute decisions or solve problems. These conditional statements are crafted from the expertise of specialists in a particular field. The system applies these rules to the input data to formulate conclusions.

The "if" segment of a statement evaluates the data for specific conditions or patterns. When these conditions are satisfied, the "then" segment is activated, performing a designated action or drawing a conclusion. Importantly, these systems do not adapt or learn from data in the manner that machine learning models do. Rather, they rely on a set of explicit rules, which are the codified versions of expert knowledge within a specific domain. This knowledge is methodically organized and stored in a knowledge base, enabling the system to reference and apply it efficiently during its operations.

In Chapter 2.3.1, we will explore the technical details and applications of rule-based systems, emphasizing their pivotal role during the rule-based era of AI's evolution.

B. Vector-Space

The vector-space model marked a significant shift, representing objects and features as vectors in a high-dimensional space. This approach facilitated the development of various distance functions to assess similarity for different applications. Notably, a comprehensive survey by [65] categorized 45 distance functions into families like inner product, L_1, Minkowski, and Intersection, each with its representative functions highlighting the versatility in vector-space analysis.

B.1. Inner product, dot product and cosine

The inner product and dot product are the same in the context of Euclidean space and are defined for vectors $\mathbf{a}$ and $\mathbf{b}$ as:

$$\mathbf{a} \cdot \mathbf{b} = a_1 b_1 + a_2 b_2 + \ldots + a_n b_n.$$

This operation results in a scalar value and indicates the vectors' magnitude and directionality.

Cosine similarity is a measure that calculates the cosine of the angle between two vectors. It is defined as the dot product of the vectors normalized by the product of their magnitudes:

$$\text{cosine similarity}(\mathbf{a}, \mathbf{b}) = \frac{\mathbf{a} \cdot \mathbf{b}}{\|\mathbf{a}\| \|\mathbf{b}\|},$$

where $\|\mathbf{a}\|$ and $\|\mathbf{b}\|$ represent the Euclidean norms of the vectors $\mathbf{a}$ and $\mathbf{b}$, respectively.

The cosine similarity is especially useful in contexts where the magnitude of the vectors is not of primary concern, making it ideal for applications in high-dimensional spaces like text analysis and information retrieval.

B.2. Weighted Minkowski

The weighted Minkowski distance function allows assigning varying importance to different dimensions, accommodating the significance of specific features in contexts like machine learning and data mining. The weighted Minkowski distance between two points $X = (x_1, x_2, \ldots, x_n)$ and $Y = (y_1, y_2, \ldots, y_n)$ with a set of weights $W = (w_1, w_2, \ldots, w_n)$ is defined as:

$$D(X,Y) = \left(\sum_{i=1}^{n} w_i |x_i - y_i|^p \right)^{\frac{1}{p}},$$

B.3. Set similarity

Moreover, the Jaccard similarity [66] provides a robust method for comparing sets, especially beneficial in scenarios where feature presence or absence is more critical than their magnitude, as seen in plagiarism or copyright detection.

$$J(X,Y) = \frac{|X \cap Y|}{|X \cup Y|}$$

Where:

- $|A \cap B|$ is the number of elements in the intersection of A and B.
- $|A \cup B|$ is the number of elements in the union of A and B.

C. Probabilistic-Based

The advancement into probabilistic-based models introduced a spectrum of statistical and probabilistic distance functions, offering refined tools for quantifying similarity or dissimilarity based on underlying probabilistic principles. These functions, including Pearson Correlation Coefficient, Mahalanobis Distance, Kullback-Leibler Divergence, and others, cater to diverse analytical needs, enriching the computational toolkit available for similarity assessment in various domains.

This section underscores the computer science perspective on similarity, detailing its journey from rule-based logic to advanced probabilistic models, reflecting the field's dynamic evolution and its pivotal role in shaping contemporary approaches to measuring similarity.

2.2.3 Cognitive Psychology Perspective

Cognitive psychology and neuroscience provide deep insights into how similarity is perceived and processed at a neural level, significantly influencing the development of AI technologies. Anne Treisman's Feature Integration Theory (FIT) [67] has been instrumental in understanding how the brain synthesizes various sensory features into cohesive percepts, a concept that has parallels in how artificial neural networks, particularly Convolutional Neural Networks (CNNs) [68, 69], process visual information.

FIT draws heavily from Gestalt psychology principles [70, 71], which propose that perception organizes individual components into a meaningful whole. This aligns with FIT's view that perception is an integrated experience shaped by the brain's organizational tendencies. The theory also intersects with selective attention, as seen in Donald Broadbent's Filter Model [72]. This model suggests attention acts as a filter, selecting relevant information for further processing. Broadbent's framework complements FIT by emphasizing attention's role in integrating features into a unified perception, highlighting the brain's selective processes.

In 2001, while conducting a study on perceptual similarity with my PhD student Beitao Li, we uncovered that images could demonstrate similarity in various dimensions. The weighted-Minkowski function, although could learn feature weights, its application was universal once the weights were set, representing a statistical average. Our experiments with transformed images–through translation, cropping, rotation, down-sampling, and affine scaling–revealed that while these images were perceptually similar to their originals, their similarities were in distinct aspects. This observation led to the development of our "Dynamic Partial Function" (DPF) in 2002 [73, 74]. The DPF signature for each image pair could be unique. Essentially, if a pair of images (or objects) demonstrates a sufficient number of similar features, they are likely deemed similar, regardless of the specific features. For instance, an image is considered similar to its rotated version due to their color histograms' similarity. Similarly, an image and its cropped version are considered alike based on their texture features. If two images exhibit a sufficient degree of similarity in various respects–typically 60%–they are generally regarded as similar.

While survey the literature, we came across "Respects for Similarity" by Medin, Goldstone, and Gentner [75], which portrays

Figure 2.1: “Which Pairs are Similar?” (DALL-E)

similarity as a dynamic process of formulating a function and identifying relevant aspects, a process that is realized consciously. To clarify this concept, let’s refer to an example from [74]:

Consider the task of identifying two places similar to England. Scotland and New England might emerge as viable candidates. Yet, the criteria making England similar to Scotland are distinct from those linking England to New England. Using the attributes that align England with Scotland to assess the similarity between England and New England might not yield a parallel conclusion, and the reverse is also true. This scenario underscores the idea that objects can be similar to a reference object in varied respects. A fixed similarity function, bound to a specific set of criteria, fails to capture the similarities across different contexts. Medin, Goldstone, and Gentner [75] examine the operational dynamics of similarity in human cognition, noting that the selection of relevant attributes is crucial, with similarity being as much a result as a driving force of conceptual coherence. Goldstone [76] further elucidates that similarity involves identifying the appropriate criteria for comparison, which occurs *only after the objects in question have been juxtaposed*, not beforehand. The criteria selected for this comparison are activated during the comparison process, with a tendency to favor those that enhance the coherence of the objects being compared.

Although the Dynamic Partial Function (DPF) introduces computational complexity, it has indirectly played a role in the success of AlexNet [77] by influencing data augmentation strategies. By integrating transformed images into its training dataset, AlexNet benefits from a principle akin to DPF, thereby improving its accuracy and robustness in recognition tasks. The recent advancements in transformer algorithms [63], which focus on dynamism and context-awareness, build on this foundation, a topic that will be explored in detail in the subsequent section.

Neuroscience

The neuroscience foundation of FIT and its relation to visual feature processing are echoed in the development of CNNs, which were inspired by the visual cortex's hierarchical structure and feature detection capabilities as explored by Hubel and Wiesel [78]. These networks utilize convolutional layers to automatically and adaptively learn spatial hierarchies of features from visual data, akin to the neural processing observed in the brain.

Techniques like Multivariate Pattern Analysis (MVPA) [79] and Neural Decoding [80] further bridge the gap between neuroscience and AI, offering methods to analyze how information is represented across neural populations and how these representations can predict perceptual experiences or cognitive states. These methodologies have inspired and informed the design of advanced AI systems, particularly in how they encode, process, and differentiate complex patterns and similarities.

The cross-pollination between neuroscience and AI, exemplified by the influence of neural processing principles on CNN design, highlights the symbiotic relationship between these fields. Insights from studying the brain's processing mechanisms have catalyzed innovations in AI, leading to more effective and biologically inspired computational models. This interdisciplinary exchange not only propels forward our understanding of neural processes but also fosters the development of AI systems that more closely mimic human perceptual and cognitive capabilities.

2.2.4 Section Remarks

The exploration of similarity measurement spans across linguistics, computer science, and cognitive psychology and neuroscience, revealing its multidisciplinary nature. Each field offers a unique lens to view similarity, from the contextual information in language, computational algorithms in AI, to the neural processing in the human brain. They converge on the common ground of representing entities in high-dimensional spaces and employing distance metrics for quantification, highlighting the universal applicability of similarity. This convergence fosters a rich dialogue between disciplines, enhancing our understanding and ability to quantify and interpret similarity, driving forward innovation and providing new methodologies that influence a wide array of contexts in our quest to decode this fundamental concept.

2.3 Eras of Similarity Measurement

Traversing through the history of artificial intelligence and similarity measurement, one can delineate distinct eras, each marked by unique methodologies and technological advancements. Contrast to last section which examines similarity measurements from different scientific disciplines, this section chronicles these eras, starting from the *rule-based* era, which laid the foundational stones, through the evolution into *model-based*, *data-centric*, and *context-aware* methodologies, illustrating the dynamic trajectory of similarity measurement in AI. As we reach the conclusion of this section, we explore the prospects of the forthcoming era, which promises to challenge and expand our understanding by venturing into the realm of discovering the *unknown unknowns*.

2.3.1 Rule-Based Era (1950s -)

The rule-based era of the 1950s marked the inception of AI, characterized by the use of symbolic representations and logic to analyze similarity. This period saw the emergence of explicit symbolic representations and logic-based methods tailored for similarity assessment. Innovations by Allen Newell and Herbert A. Simon with tools like the Logic Theorist and General Problem Solver [81] pioneered logical rule-based problem solving, setting a pivotal foundation for AI's evolution.

In the following decades, systems such as DENDRAL [82] utilized rule-based logic to deduce molecular structures from data, while MYCIN [83], an expert system for diagnosing infections and recommending treatments, demonstrated the practical application of rule-based reasoning in the field of medical diagnostics.

Despite their effectiveness in well-defined scenarios, rule-based systems have limitations in more complex or changing environments. However, their clarity and systematic nature are invaluable in certain applied areas, for example:

1. *Customer Service*: Rule-based chatbots are prevalent in customer service, using predefined rules to respond to inquiries based on detected keywords or phrases in user input, providing immediate and consistent customer support.

2. *Fraud Detection Systems*: The finance sector employs rule-based systems to identify potential fraudulent transactions by comparing against specific criteria, such as unusual transaction amounts or atypical locations.

3. *Equipment Failure Diagnosis*: In industrial settings, rule-based systems analyze data to pinpoint causes of equipment failures, leveraging historical data and expert knowledge to predict and prevent future breakdowns.

This era introduced key tools like PROLOG [84] for logic programming and decision trees [85] for visualizing decision processes, exemplifying rule-based logic.

While rule-based systems initially approached similarity with a clear, logical framework, subsequent AI advancements have embraced more flexible methods like statistical models and machine learning, offering a broader, more adaptable approach to understanding similarity in various contexts.

Rule-based systems contrast with the "black-box" nature of current Convolutional Neural Networks (CNNs) and Large Language Models (LLMs) in terms of interpretability and decision-making processes. Rule-based systems are transparent in how decisions are made, as they follow a clear set of if-then rules or logic for inference, allowing users to understand and trace the reasoning behind each decision.

On the other hand, CNNs and LLMs, particularly those based on deep learning, often operate as black boxes, where the internal decision-making processes are not easily interpretable. In these systems, decisions result from complex, non-linear interactions of thousands to millions of parameters that have been adjusted through the learning process. While they are powerful and effective in handling a wide range of tasks, especially those involving large datasets and requiring pattern recognition beyond human capabilities, their inner workings are not as transparent or interpretable as rule-based systems.

2.3.2 Model-Based Era (1970s -)

In this era, vector-space and probabilistic models were designed to quantify similarity.

2.3.2.1 Vector Space Models

The vector-space era marked a shift in similarity measurement from rule-based to representation-based approaches. In this era, objects, documents, and features began to be conceptualized as vectors in a high-dimensional space, fostering a more intuitive and flexible method for assessing similarity.

The Vector-Space Model and Information Retrieval

At the core of this era was the vector-space model, which represents documents as vectors of term frequencies, enabling the computation of document similarity using cosine similarity between their respective vectors. This model enhanced the efficiency and effectiveness of information retrieval systems.

Distance Functions and Feature Weighting

A diverse array of distance functions emerged during this era to quantify the similarity between vectors. The Minkowski distance, for instance, generalized traditional metrics like the Euclidean and Manhattan distances, offering flexibility in adjusting the sensitivity to differences in vector components. Weighted distance measures also gained prominence, recognizing that not all features have equal importance in similarity assessment. The weighted Minkowski distance, in particular, allowed for differential weighting of dimensions based on their relevance to the specific application at hand.

Beyond Textual Data

The utility of the vector-space model extended well beyond textual data. In the realm of image processing, features (e.g., colors, textures, and shapes) extracted from images were represented as vectors, enabling the assessment of image similarity based on the distances between these vectors. This paradigm facilitated significant advancements in image retrieval, classification, and clustering.

Dimensionality Reduction Techniques

To address the challenges posed by high-dimensional data, techniques like Principal Component Analysis (PCA) [86] and Latent

Semantic Analysis (LSA) [87] were developed. These methods reduced the dimensionality of data while preserving its essential structure, enhancing computational efficiency and mitigating the "curse of dimensionality." Manifold learning, a non-linear dimension reduction approach, further expanded the toolbox for tackling high-dimensional data [88]. For a comprehensive overview of these techniques, refer to [89].

The vector-space era laid the groundwork for advancements in machine learning and data mining, making similarity measures essential for clustering, classification, and recommendation systems. Data representation as vectors allowed for the exploration of relationships across varied data types through the nearest neighbor concept. In this context, the characteristics or labels of an unknown instance's k-nearest neighbors could be inferred and applied to the instance, with these neighbors determined by distance metrics.

However, vector representations often result in sparsity, potentially leading to resource inefficiency and decreased accuracy. These models, while capturing syntactic relationships, sometimes struggle with semantic depth, such as identifying synonyms or contextual meaning. The assumption of feature independence and the use of linear methods in dimensionality reduction can also lead to inaccuracies, particularly with non-linear data structures. The introduction of Support Vector Machines (SVMs) [90], which utilize kernel methods, addressed some challenges related to non-linear data but increased computational complexity. SVMs were a significant focus in the field until the rise of deep learning architectures like AlexNet marked a shift towards the data-centric era.

2.3.2.2 Probabilistic Models

Probabilistic models offer more flexibility than vector-space models because they can incorporate uncertainty and variability directly into their mathematical frameworks, allowing for a more comprehensive and adaptive representation of data.

Statistical Inference and Similarity

Probabilistic models introduced the concept of statistical inference, where the likelihood of data or feature occurrences was used to estimate similarity. This allowed for effective handling of uncertainty and variability in data, making it particularly useful in noisy or incomplete datasets.

Bayesian Approaches

Bayesian methods emerged as a fundamental component of this era, providing a robust framework for integrating prior knowledge and empirical data. These methods enhance model adaptability by systematically updating beliefs in light of new evidence, allowing for similarity measures that are responsive to evolving data landscapes.

For further reading on Bayesian methods and their application in dynamic and adaptive modeling, consult the following literature [91, 92, 93, 94].

Latent Semantic Models

In addressing the challenges of high dimensionality and data sparsity inherent in vector-space models, dimensionality reduction techniques were employed. However, beyond merely tackling these issues, the development of a latent semantic layer offered profound implications for semantic analysis and indexing.

As highlighted in the perspective section (Chapter 2.2), Latent Semantic Analysis (LSA) [59] and Latent Dirichlet Allocation

(LDA) [60] are critical models in the landscape of semantic modeling. LSA employs singular value decomposition to condense the dimensionality of term-document matrices, unveiling the latent semantic structures within textual data. This dimensional reduction elucidates intricate relationships beyond mere surface-level feature overlaps, enabling a deeper comprehension of textual similarities.

Figure 2.2: Latent Clusters of LDA. The words in red belong to two semantic clusters, signifying the meaning of a word depends on its context.

Similarly, LDA offers a probabilistic approach to topic modeling, where documents are considered mixtures of various topics, and topics are distributions over words. This bag-of-words model facilitates a deeper semantic connection between documents by associating them based on shared topics rather than just overlapping terms.

Figure 2.2 presents an example of how LDA, through its bag-of-words approach, clusters words into semantic groups. It's noteworthy that a word can belong to multiple semantic clusters. For instance, words like 'characters', 'play', 'court', 'evidence', and 'test', each appears in two different semantic clusters in the illustration. This feature of LDA resonates with the insights from Zellig Harris's pioneering work and John R. Firth's adage that "A word is known by the company it keeps."

These latent semantic models transcend the limitations of direct feature comparison, enabling a more abstract representation of text. By doing so, they provide a robust foundation for semantic indexing and similarity assessment, offering insights that are essential for tasks such as information retrieval, document clustering, and topic discovery. The adoption of these models marked a significant advancement in understanding and measuring similarity in text, setting a new standard for semantic analysis in the field of natural language processing.

Cluster Analysis and Similarity

Probabilistic clustering algorithms, like Gaussian Mixture Models (GMMs), leveraged statistical methods to group data based on the likelihood of membership in different clusters. This probabilistic approach provided a more flexible and deeper understanding of groupings and similarities within data.

Impact and Limitations

While probabilistic models brought significant advancements, they also introduced challenges. The increased complexity often led to higher computational demands. Additionally, reliance on assumptions about data distributions or the need for prior knowledge could limit applicability in certain situations.

The probabilistic model expanded the toolkit for measuring similarity by introducing methods that could handle uncertainty and offer more adaptive and context-aware approaches. These advancements paved the way for even more sophisticated techniques in the subsequent data-centric era, where the focus shifted towards leveraging vast amounts of data to learn and adapt similarity measures dynamically.

2.3.3 Data-Centric Era (2000s -)

The data-centric era marked a transformative shift in artificial intelligence, pivoting towards harnessing the vast potential of big data, enabled by advances in computational hardware that facilitated parallel processing. This era is characterized by a move from heuristic-based methods to an empirical, data-driven approach in feature representation and model learning.

At the core of the data-centric paradigm is the emphasis on deriving model parameters from extensive datasets, distinguishing it from traditional model-centric strategies. Foundational algorithms such as CNNs [49] and Transformers [63], while conceived through human ingenuity, saw their efficacy significantly enhanced when trained on large, diverse datasets. This training ensures broad coverage of potential variations across different objects or concepts, fortifying the models' ability to accurately recognize and classify new instances. The volume and diversity of the training data are crucial in refining the models' representations, leading to advancements in prediction accuracy and robustness.

From MapReduce to Machine Learning at Scale

The inception of the data-centric movement traces back to the seminal works in statistical learning theory. Vladimir Vapnik's insights into the importance of data for model generalization, particularly his development of Support Vector Machines (SVMs) [90], and Tom Mitchell's pivotal book "Machine Learning" [95], which underscored the critical role of data in preventing overfitting, laid the theoretical foundation for this era.

MapReduce [96], a corner stone in data processing, enabled parallel computation to efficiently handle large datasets. Originally devised to enhance data processing tasks like Google's web indexing, MapReduce became the bedrock for the emergence of sophisticated data-centric methodologies in AI.

Evolution of Machine Learning with Big Data

The rise of parallel machine learning algorithms [97, 50, 98], notably through Edward Y. Chang's work at Google, marked a significant milestone in this era. Chang and his team pioneered Web-scale image annotation in 2007 [50], and subsequently met Prof. Fei-Fei Li after 2028 summer school of Computer Vision, and subsequently sponsored the Stanford ImageNet [58] work via a substantial Google grant.

At the same time, his team developed groundbreaking parallel algorithms, including PSVM [99] (parallelizing SVMs by approximating matrix factorization), PFP [100] (parallelizing frequent itemset mining), PLDA [101] (parallelizing LDA algorithm), PSC [102] (parallelizing spectral clustering), and SpeeDo [103] (parallelizing CNNs), driven by the recognition that big data could facilitate direct learning of features and representations, transcending the limitations of human-crafted heuristics.

Impact on Similarity Measurement

The data-centric era revolutionized the field of similarity measurement, ushering in a new paradigm where similarity metrics are derived from extensive datasets. This period underscored the critical role of data volume and quality in defining similarity metrics, highlighting the dynamic relationship between data-driven insights and computational methods.

In this era, deep learning architectures like CNNs and Transformers have been instrumental in advancing similarity metrics. These models stand out because they not only adjust feature weights but also autonomously learn features from the data. This capability to learn from data directly makes traditional human-engineered features increasingly redundant. After all, human heuristics may not capture every facet of an object or concept comprehensively, and human sensory perception is limited. For instance, while humans can detect the light spectrum from approximately 300 to 700 nanometers, cameras and X-ray machines can perceive a broader range of signals, demonstrating the advantage of machine-learned features in capturing and analyzing data beyond human limitations.

2.3.4 Context-Aware Era (2010s -)

The context-aware era in similarity measurement brings to fruition the profound insights of Zellig Harris's distributional semantics and John R. Firth's adage: "a word is known by the company it keeps." This period marks a shift from static, context-independent assessments to dynamic, context-informed interpretations of similarity. It utilizes the latest advancements in machine learning and the growing availability of computational power to enhance our understanding of similarity in various contexts.

Emergence and Evolution

The integration of context-aware methodologies in similarity measurement evolved significantly in the 2010s, overcoming earlier constraints in computational power and data availability:

- *Computation Capacity*: The development of AlexNet encouraged a data-centric focus within the AI community, prompting investments in parallel computing infrastructures.
- *Word Embeddings*: Techniques like Word2Vec enhanced semantic relationship encoding within data.
- *Attention Models and Transformers*: These models improved data analysis by concentrating on relevant data segments, refining context-aware assessments.
- *Large Language Models (LLMs)*: Models such as BERT and GPT, utilizing self-supervised learning on large text corpora, improved the understanding and generation of context-rich text.

Foundational Pillars: Data and Computation

Key pillars supported advancements in the context-aware era:

- *Self-Supervised Learning:* Utilizing unlabeled data for learning enabled models to extract insights from the data, improving AI system efficiency and scalability.
- *Computational Advances:* The introduction of parallel algorithms and GPU acceleration enabled processing at unprecedented scales, facilitating the development of sophisticated models.

Broader Implications

This era not only refined similarity measurement techniques but also broadened how data is understood and knowledge is integrated:

- *Reasoning and Explanation:* Models now aim to provide reasons for their similarity assessments, improving interpretability and building trust.
- *Multilinguality and Cultural Sensitivity:* Enhanced processing capabilities for varied linguistic and cultural data improve the global applicability of similarity measurements.
- *Multimodal Data Integration:* Context-aware models are adept at combining information from multiple modalities, offering a comprehensive view of similarity.
- *Polydisciplinary Knowledge Fusion:* Adopting a polydisciplinary approach allows for a broader knowledge base in making similarity assessments, fostering innovation across different fields.

The context-aware era signifies a shift toward more insightful, holistic, and interpretable AI, setting the stage for future developments where AI can offer contextually rich and multifaceted insights.

2.3.5 Section Remarks

What defines the next era in the evolution of AI? Historically, technological advancements have focused on addressing pressing unmet needs. Among various potential areas, enhancing the interpretability of decisions stands out as a crucial objective. Making the decision-making process of LLMs transparent and explainable could unlock significant improvements in numerous aspects, such as ethics, by enabling foundational enhancements rather than superficial tweaks based on guesswork and simple heuristics.

The fusion of rule-based system interpretability with the sophisticated capabilities of CNNs and LLMs poses a compelling challenge in AI. Active research is aimed at blending these approaches to leverage their distinct advantages:

1. *Neuro-Symbolic AI*: Neuro-Symbolic AI (the third wave of AI [104]) aims to blend the data processing power of neural networks with the logical reasoning of symbolic AI. The goal is to create systems that not only excel in tasks like pattern recognition but can also reason and make decisions in a human-interpretable manner.

2. *Incorporating Domain Knowledge*: Embedding knowledge of experts within neural networks [105] can steer the learning process towards more reliable and interpretable outcomes. In healthcare, for example, integrating medical guidelines into the training process of a neural network ensures that its predictions for patient treatment not only correlate with the data but also align with established medical practices, enhancing both the model's credibility and relevance.

3. *Interactive Systems*: A system such as SocraSynth [4] can combine the predictive power of deep neural networks with human expertise, allowing for iterative refinement and learning. For instance, in SocraHealth [33], it might suggest a set of possible diagnoses based on medical imaging, which a physician could then refine or correct. This feedback could be used to continuously improve the system, marrying machine efficiency with human expertise to enhance decision accuracy and interpretability.

By advancing these strategies, the field of AI aims to develop models that not only excel in performance but are also transparent, understandable, and aligned with human reasoning, thus making AI more reliable and trustworthy across various applications.

2.4 Concluding Remarks

This chapter examines the history of AI through the lens of similarity, considering both disciplinary and chronological perspectives. Looking forward, we propose that the emergence of large language models (LLMs) marks a pivotal moment in the context-aware era of AI, setting the stage for the next frontier: the era of interpretability, understanding, and discovery. In this new era, the focus will shift towards empowering LLMs to not only comprehend but also to generate and innovate, synthesizing novel knowledge and insights.

This era of discovery is envisioned as a time when machines will extend their superiority beyond mastering games like Go and Chess to encompass a broader spectrum of tasks, outstripping human capabilities in various domains. The subsequent chapters of this book, beginning with Chapter 6, explore the concept of harnessing the collective intelligence of multiple LLMs, embarking on a voyage to transcend the boundaries of the known and venture into the realm of discovery.

This chapter has explored the history of AI through the lenses of disciplinary and chronological perspectives, focusing on the concept of similarity. As we look to the future, the rise of large language models (LLMs) marks a significant milestone in the context-aware era, paving the way for a new era focused on interpretability, comprehension, and exploration. The upcoming phase in AI's evolution emphasizes enhancing LLMs with the ability to not just generate but also interpret and innovate, pushing the boundaries of knowledge creation and insight synthesis.

We anticipate an era where AI's capability extends beyond excelling in strategic games like Go and Chess to a wider array of endeavors, surpassing human performance across multiple fields. The following chapters, starting with Chapter 6, research deeply into leveraging the collective intelligence of various LLMs. This journey aims to explore uncharted territories, advancing beyond established knowledge to uncover new frontiers in artificial intelligence.

3 Capabilities and Opportunities of LLMs

Abstract

This chapter describes the architectural innovations and unique capabilities of Large Language Models (LLMs), with a special emphasis on the GPT-4 model. We dissect GPT-4's salient characteristics, such as its extensive cross-disciplinary and multimodal data representation, the intricate balance in its training methodologies, and the harmonious integration of human-guided insights with a robust data-driven learning framework. The chapter highlights the potential of LLMs to not only comprehend, but also synthesize knowledge that transcends their training datasets, venturing into realms potentially uncharted by human understanding. We postulate that the true potential of LLMs is significantly dependent on the articulation of the queries posed to them. By elucidating these aspects, the chapter aims to shed light on how LLMs could rival or even surpass human intelligence in certain knowledge domains, setting a foundation for the subsequent exploration of LLMs' characteristics, insights, and their implications for future AI advancements.

Introduction

The evolution of large language models (LLMs) [106, 107, 108, 109, 110] has significantly influenced natural language processing, enhancing the capabilities in machine translation, sentiment analysis, and text summarization. Among these, GPT-4 [108] stands out for its exemplary performance on various benchmarks, including MMLU [111]. Despite its achievements, GPT-4 is faced with challenges such as hallucination, bias, and restricted reasoning.

This chapter studies the deep intricacies of GPT-4's architecture, emphasizing its knowledge representation, alignment with human values, and the synergy between human insights and data-driven learning. We discuss the limitations of the model and introduce SocraSynth, a supplementary reasoning layer designed to enhance knowledge discovery and analytical reasoning in GPT-4 and similar LLMs.

Capabilities and Implications

We explore the architecture of GPT-4, which, although initially kept in secrecy, has been progressively unveiled by the research community [112, 113, 114]. Our focus is on the representation and discovery of knowledge, alignment with human values, and the integration of human expertise with data-centric methodologies.

Collaborations between Microsoft and OpenAI [106] highlight the interdisciplinary approach of GPT-4 and the benchmark achievements of its polymodal variant. We will further explore these aspects in Chapter 15. Discussions on human-value or ethical alignment and the implications of pre-training censorship on foundational models, detailed in Chapter 10.

Limitations and Opportunities

Addressing the biases, hallucinations, and constrained reasoning of LLMs requires innovative research initiatives. We introduce four key areas of focus:

- Enhancing Collaborative LLMs with Theoretical Foundations in Statistics and Information Theory.
- Employing Open-Domain Reasoning with the Socratic Method to Guide LLMs.
- Model behavioral emotion to protect AI safety and ethics.
- Implementing Retrospective and Adaptive Evolving Learning Frameworks to Refine LLMs.

The root of bias in Large Language Models (LLMs) often lies in their training data. Based on the transformer architecture, LLMs prioritize accurate token prediction, relying heavily on statistical patterns within their training corpus. This can inadvertently lead to bias towards prevalent opinions and expressions. To address this, Chapter 6 introduces SocraSynth, a framework designed to challenge these statistical tendencies by pitting two LLM agents against each other on a topic, each conditioned with opposing viewpoints. Chapter 7 builds on this by developing theoretical pillars to measure, monitor and manage multi-LLM dialogue, thus improving prediction quality and stability.

Chapters 7, 8 and the online chapters listed in the appendix demonstrate SocraSynth' effectiveness in mitigating biases across various domains, showcasing its adaptability and efficiency in complex decision-making scenarios. Its application in fields such as disease diagnosis, content bias correction, corporate sales strategy, and geopolitical analysis exemplifies the potential of SocraSynth to provide context-aware solutions.

Chapters 9 and 10 delve into the intricate relationship between emotions and linguistic behaviors in AI. Chapter 9 focuses on modeling emotions expressed in written text and by LLMs, while Chapter 10 examines how these linguistic behaviors can be mapped to a set of emotions, ensuring ethical considerations in AI development.

Chapter 13 shifts focus to consciousness modeling, presenting a proposed architecture and mechanism for its implementation, moving beyond mere computation. Chapter 14 addresses knowledge deficiencies and hallucinations in LLMs, often stemming from suboptimal query formulation and insufficient knowledge. While SocraSynth tackles the former, Chapter 14 introduces RAFEL, a framework designed to diagnose poorly answered questions and recommend relevant information sources for effective Retrieval-Augmented Generation (RAG). Chapter 15 concludes with an illustrative example showcasing the potential of LLMs to discover knowledge that may be beyond human reach, utilizing the methods presented in this book.

4 Prompt Engineering: Few Shots, Chain of Thought, and Retrieval-Augmented Generation

Abstract This chapter presents the significance of prompt engineering in the context of Large Language Models (LLMs), particularly focusing on OpenAI's GPT series. Prompt engineering involves crafting text inputs (prompts) that guide LLMs to generate desired outputs, a practice that gained traction with the advent of GPT-2 and GPT-3 and further emphasized with ChatGPT. The chapter discusses how a well-constructed prompt, rich in contextual information, increases the likelihood of eliciting accurate responses, drawing parallels with information retrieval principles. It also introduces Retrieval-Augmented Generation (RAG), which enhances response quality by integrating relevant external data into the generative process. Additionally, the chapter categorizes prompts into five types based on detail and iteration levels and examines the evolution of RAG, assessing its benefits and potential to overcome context window limitations.

Introduction

In the realm of Large Language Models (LLMs), the concept of a "prompt" has gained prominence, particularly with the introduction of OpenAI's GPT series. The term became widespread around 2018 and 2019 following the release of GPT-2 and GPT-3.

When interacting with these LLMs, a user inputs a piece of text (the prompt), prompting the model to generate a corresponding response. The emergence of "prompt engineering" or "prompt design" refers to the strategies employed to construct prompts that effectively steer the model toward generating the intended output, a practice that has become particularly useful with the advent of ChatGPT.

To increase the probability of eliciting a desired response, a prompt must be rich in information. This concept is akin to the principles of information retrieval services, where a user must clearly articulate their intent and context to obtain pertinent information. This process depends on the service's "data availability" and its capabilities in information matching and retrieval. In the sphere of prompt engineering, the responsibility for generating high-quality, targeted outputs rests on the user's ability to supply comprehensive and precise information through the prompt. As a result, the craft of prompt formulation and engineering has become an optimization endeavor: deciding on the most effective information to incorporate to enhance output quality, considering the model's knowledge base and interaction protocols.

Data availability, as previously highlighted, is crucial to information retrieval. If the desired information is absent, the prompt's effectiveness is naturally constrained, leading to unsatisfactory results. Retrieval-Augmented Generation (RAG) is instrumental in this context, as it identifies, retrieves, and incorporates pertinent external data into the generative process, enhancing the response's accuracy and relevance. Consequently, prompt engineering and RAG synergistically enhance the model's response quality and relevance.

5 CRIT: Socratic Inquiry for Critical Thinking in LLMs

Abstract This chapter presents a systematic approach to using the Socratic method in developing prompt templates that effectively interact with large language models, including GPT-3. Various methods are examined, and those that yield precise answers and justifications while fostering creativity and imagination to enhance creative writing are identified. Techniques such as *definition*, *elenchus*, *dialectic*, *maieutics*, *generalization*, and *counterfactual reasoning* are discussed for their application in engineering prompt templates and their connections to inductive, deductive, and abductive reasoning. Through examples, the effectiveness of these dialogue and reasoning methods is demonstrated. An interesting observation is made that when the task's goal and user intent are conveyed to GPT-3 via ChatGPT before the start of a dialogue, the large language model seems to connect to the external context expressed in the intent and perform more effectively.

Introduction

Prompting is a technique used to guide the output generation of a pre-trained language model such as GPT-3 [115]. This is achieved by providing input in the form of a question or template, which helps to generate specific responses such as Q&A, document summarization, and translations. The advent of ChatGPT [116, 107, 117] has revolutionized the field of NLP by demonstrating the potential of using large pre-trained language models with prompting. Despite this progress, there is still room for improvement in current prompting strategies and techniques, especially for specific target applications. In this study, we investigate the Socratic method [118, 119] to identify and evaluate potential prompting strategies, and use the findings to design effective prompt templates.

Traditional NLP tasks involve various sub-tasks, such as named entity recognition, dependency parsing, coreference resolution [120], semantic parsing [121, 122], and more, to comprehend the meaning of a sentence. By utilizing prompt templates with large language models (LLMs), these sub-tasks can be delegated to the LLM, freeing the template to focus specifically on dialogue design. In this regard, the Socratic method [123] holds significant relevance, as it is well-known for using questioning (prompting) as a means of promoting critical thinking and delving into complex concepts [124].

The Socratic method has a long history of being regarded as the basis of critical thinking. However, some recent studies have cast doubt on its effectiveness in practice. In his paper "Socratic Irony and Argumentation," Airaksinen [125] criticizes the method for its rigidly defined roles of teacher and student, which can lead to fear of not meeting the teacher's expectations and reluctance to participate. Similarly, Stoddard's "The Use of Socratic Questioning in Clinical Teaching" [126] highlights the risk of the method being misused in a manner that lacks psychological safety for students. Fortunately, when using the Socratic method in a dialogue with an LLM, the absence of emotions and sarcasm, as well as the option to deactivate the model, can alleviate many of the problems associated with human interaction.

This study starts by presenting an overview of the Socratic method's strategies and techniques. To begin, we list ten widely referenced methods [127] under the Socratic method umbrella and use hypothesis elimination to identify the most relevant ones for our goal of prompt-template development. The selected methods are definition, hypothesis elimination, elenchus, dialectic, maieutics, generalization, and induction. Furthermore, we add to the list counterfactual reasoning, which is a concept in logic that involves considering what might have happened if a particular event had occurred differently. We then perform experiments using GPT-3 to test and evaluate these methods, and offer suggestions for incorporating these strategies and techniques into prompt templates.

In their work on "Critical Thinking: The Art of Socratic Questioning," Paul and Elder identify three types of Socratic questioning: spontaneous, exploratory, and focused [128]. We will not discuss spontaneous questioning, as it is similar to casual conversation. Focused questioning (type 2), on the other hand, is geared towards gaining knowledge and truth, and methods such as *definition*, *elenchus* (cross-examination), *hypothesis elimination*, *dialectic*, and *generalization* hold great potential for developing effective prompting strategies and improving the response accuracy of a large language model (LLM). An interesting observation is that when the user intent is conveyed to GPT-3 during the task *definition* stage, before the start of a dialogue, the LLM seems to connect to the external context expressed in the intent and perform more effectively.

Additionally, exploratory thinking (type 3) can be supported through the *maieutics* (midwife) method, *induction*, and *counter-*

factual reasoning, which can guide GPT-3 towards producing imaginative and creative writing. While many of the plot suggestions generated by GPT-3's exploration may not be useful, a few unique recommendations in response to a "what if" query can stimulate the writer's imagination and lead to remarkable results. When applied effectively, these methods can turn an LLM into a writer's muse, providing inspiration and guiding the creative process [129].

The main contributions of this chapter are as follows:

- An overview of the Socratic method's strategies, their evaluation, and selection of the most relevant ones for the development of effective prompt templates.
- An examination of how the definition, elenchus, hypothesis elimination, dialectic, and generalization methods can improve the output's accuracy and conciseness through clarification and verification.
- An illustration of how maieutics, induction, and counterfactual reasoning can foster productive generalization and creativity.

6 SocraSynth: Adversarial Multi-LLM Reasoning

Abstract Large language models (LLMs), while promising, face criticisms for biases, hallucinations, and a lack of reasoning capability. This chapter introduces SocraSynth, a multi-LLM agent reasoning platform developed to mitigate these issues. SocraSynth utilizes conditional statistics and systematic context enhancement through continuous arguments, alongside adjustable debate contentiousness levels. The platform typically involves a human moderator and two LLM agents representing opposing viewpoints on a given subject. SocraSynth operates in two main phases: knowledge generation and reasoning evaluation. In the knowledge generation phase, the moderator defines the debate topic and contentiousness level, prompting the agents to formulate supporting arguments for their respective stances. The reasoning evaluation phase then employs Socratic reasoning and formal logic principles to appraise the quality of the arguments presented. The dialogue concludes with the moderator adjusting the contentiousness from confrontational to collaborative, gathering final, conciliatory remarks to aid in human reasoning and decision-making. Through case studies in two distinct application domains, this chapter highlights SocraSynth's effectiveness in fostering rigorous research, dynamic reasoning, comprehensive assessment, and enhanced collaboration.

Introduction

Revolutionary advancements in large language models (LLMs) [106, 107, 130, 109, 110], and more broadly, foundation models (FMs) [131], have set the stage for significant progress in multi-agent systems, particularly in knowledge acquisition and natural language understanding [132]. As detailed in sources like [106, 4, 108], models such as GPT-4 exhibit extraordinary information processing capabilities. These include deep and extensive knowledge, interdisciplinary assimilation and fusion of knowledge, and multimodal and multilingual expertise (Chapter 3).

Despite these promising developments, LLMs face challenges such as biases [133, 134], hallucinations [135], and limited reasoning capabilities [136]. In response, we introduce SocraSynth, a pioneering platform that stands for "Socratic Synthesis" or "Socratic Symposium." It encourages collaboration between humans and LLM agents, fostering the generation of deep questions and surpassing typical constraints in human reasoning, validation, and assessment.

In a standard SocraSynth setup, a human moderator pairs with two LLM agents holding opposing views. For example, one agent might argue for regulating AI, while the other opposes such regulation. An agent can be based on LLMs like GPT-4 [106], Gemini [130], or Llama [110]. The human moderator sets the debate's thematic boundaries but does not directly influence content generation, maintaining impartiality.

SocraSynth operates in two phases: the generative and the evaluative. The generative phase involves LLM agents developing and countering arguments within the moderator-defined subject until a comprehensive conclusion is reached. The evaluative phase uses diverse virtual judges, each powered by a distinct LLM, to impartially assess the debate. The Critical Inquisitive Template (CRIT) algorithm [5], based on Socratic reasoning [125, 128, 119, 118], is the evaluative cornerstone.

Three mechanisms help SocraSynth effectively mitigate biases and hallucinations and improve reasoning quality: conditional statistics, modulating debate with contentiousness, and context refinement.

Conditional Statistics

Both LLMs and Internet search engines confront biases originating from different sources. LLMs, influenced by training data, exhibit biases in next-token prediction. Search engines, through algorithms like PageRank [137] and Google NavBoost [138], rank pages based on popularity metrics like clicks and links.

SocraSynth counteracts these biases by placing two LLM agents at opposing ends of a subject matter. This approach "artificially" biases the LLMs, compelling them to break free from default model biases. Each agent adjusts its next-token generation statistics to align with its assigned stance in the debate.

Modulating Debate with Contentiousness

Contentiousness (or adversary), a key debate parameter, influences the likelihood of disagreement or argument. SocraSynth tunes contentiousness between 70% and 90% in the generative phase to provoke polarized arguments. As the debate evolves, the contentiousness level is reduced to about 50%, moderating the intensity and encouraging more focused discussions. After the generative phase, contentiousness drops to 10%, promoting a conciliatory dialogue where LLMs do not have to agree but are expected to present comprehensive arguments. These debates offer rich insights often missed in conventional searches, LLM outputs, or in environments where dissenting opinions are suppressed.

Refine Context to Mitigate Hallucinations

To address hallucinations, where LLMs generate irrelevant or nonsensical content, SocraSynth uses iterative dialogue rounds to refine the debate's context. This dynamic interaction significantly reduces irrelevant responses, ensuring that each input is continuously checked and challenged.

The CRIT algorithm's assessment of reasonableness [5] during the debate is critical. It employs the Socratic method to evaluate each argument's logic and source credibility. The human mediator or the SocraSynth algorithm then provides targeted feedback to the LLM agents, refining their reasoning capabilities.

The remainder of this chapter explores SocraSynth's architecture, algorithms, and real-world applications in detail. The key contributions of this chapter include:

1. The introduction of the SocraSynth framework, which enhances interdisciplinary reasoning with LLMs and incorporates unique algorithmic elements like conditional statistics for balanced argument generation.

2. A comprehensive exploration of SocraSynth's contentiousness modulation algorithm, a vital feature for dynamically adjusting debate intensity, enabling a spectrum of interactions from confrontational to collaborative.

3. The implementation of context refinement within SocraSynth, which continually improves the relevance and accuracy of arguments produced by LLM agents, thus elevating the overall quality of discourse.

4. The development and integration of the reasonableness evaluation mechanism, crucial for assessing the logical soundness and source credibility of arguments, thereby ensuring the integrity and utility of the discussions.

SocraSynth's applications span various fields, including geopolitical analysis [139], medical diagnostics [33], sales strategy [140], and Wikipedia article enhancement [141]. These applications demonstrate expanded perspectives and enhanced argumentation quality, along with significant reductions in biases and hallucinations, thereby demonstrating SocraSynth's efficacy in fostering balanced and well-reasoned discourse.

7 EVINCE: Optimizing Adversarial LLM Dialogues via Conditional Statistics and Information Theory

Abstract This chapter introduces EVINCE (Entropy and Variation IN Conditional Exchanges), a dialogue framework advancing Artificial General Intelligence (AGI) by enhancing versatility, adaptivity, and reasoning in large language models (LLMs). Leveraging adversarial debate and a novel dual entropy theory, EVINCE improves prediction accuracy, robustness, and stability in LLMs by integrating statistical modeling, information theory, and machine learning to balance diverse perspective exploration with strong prior exploitation. The framework's effectiveness is demonstrated through consistent convergence of information-theoretic metrics, particularly improved mutual information, fostering LLM collaboration intelligence (LCI). We apply EVINCE to healthcare, showing improved disease diagnosis, and discuss its broader implications for decision-making across domains.

Introduction

The pursuit of Artificial General Intelligence (AGI) remains a central goal of AI research. We propose a paradigm shift in this quest: utilizing multiple Large Language Models (LLMs) engaged in synergistic dialogues as a crucial step towards AGI. This approach, we contend, addresses key limitations of current AI systems and provides a novel pathway to more robust, versatile, and capable artificial intelligence. Specifically, our work targets three core AGI characteristics: versatility, iterative adaptivity, and reasoning capability.

Current LLMs, despite their remarkable capabilities, face significant challenges, including hallucination (generating false or nonsensical information), bias (reflecting and potentially amplifying societal prejudices), and limited reasoning (difficulties in complex problem-solving and logical inference). We posit that multi-agent dialogue systems offer a promising avenue to address these challenges. By fostering diversity and debate among LLMs, these systems can mitigate biases and promote enhanced reasoning capabilities. Furthermore, the *iterative nature* of multi-round dialogues allows for continuous context enrichment, enabling LLMs to access more precise information and formulate more accurate responses, thus reducing the occurrence of hallucinations.

Previous work, in particular SocraSynth [4], addresses LLM limitations through structured multi-agent dialogues. Different from treating multiple LLMs as an ensemble of experts [142, 143, 144, 145, 146] and merely taking advantage of error diversity [147] to improve respond quality, SocraSynth distinguishes itself from traditional ensemble methods by prioritizing the generation of diverse predictions over the mere avoidance of errors. This is achieved through a dynamic protocol that adaptively adjusts the "contentiousness" level of the debate, encouraging models to initially explore a wide range of perspectives and rigorously assess the quality of arguments. By leveraging both adversarial and collaborative interactions between LLMs, SocraSynth demonstrates quantifiable improvements across various domains, including healthcare [33], sales planning [140], and emotional behavior modeling [26]. These results highlight the potential for advancing towards AGI's generalized problem-solving capabilities.

While effective, SocraSynth relies on a qualitative measure of "contentiousness" to moderate LLM linguistic behaviors. For instance, a high contentiousness value (0.9 out of 1.0) might lead LLMs to challenge each other's assumptions and propose alternative solutions, while a low value (below 0.3) could encourage them to synthesize their viewpoints and find common ground. While the concept of contentiousness has proven useful in guiding SocraSynth dialogues, its qualitative nature limits its precision and explainability. In this work, we propose three theoretical pillars to quantify "contentiousness" and moderate dialogues based on statistical and information theories. These pillars, collectively referred to as EVINCE (Entropy and Variation IN Conditional Exchanges), provide quantitative measures for justifiable and explainable multi-agent dialogue moderation and evaluation:

1. *Inclusiveness Exploration*: We develop methods to ensure dialogues explore all potential perspectives. We use conditional statistics to "free" an LLM agent from its default "maximum likelihood" next-token prediction behavior, allowing it to adopt specific stances. We introduce a dual entropy optimality theory to balance the exploration of new ideas with adherence to priors, thus optimizing information exchange between agents for comprehensive and stable discourse.

2. *Information Flow Dynamics*: We introduce information theory-based metrics to quantify and optimize dialogue dynamics. These measure information diversity (entropy), novelty (statistical divergence scores), and inter-agent persuasion (mutual information). These metrics enable us to assess and enhance the quality and efficiency of information flow within the multi-agent system, fostering rich and productive exchanges.

3. *Reasoning Quality and Coherence*: We establish frameworks to assess the logical structure and coherence of multi-agent reasoning. This pillar evaluates argument validity, analytical depth, and dialogue coherence. We synergistically integrate the CRIT algorithm [5], which combines Socratic methods with formal reasoning techniques, enhances our ability to conduct critical thinking through evaluating argument quality, information-source credibility, and overall "reasonableness" within the dialogue. This integration ensures that the collective reasoning of LLM agents is not only diverse but also logically sound and aligned with the dialogue's objectives.

The core strength of EVINCE in advancing towards AGI lies in their ability to enhance key AGI characteristics through multi-agent dialogues. By employing conditional statistics and information theory, they boost versatility and adaptivity, allowing LLMs to transcend their typical "maximum likelihood" behaviors and mimic how humans adapt their linguistic behaviors to complete tasks. The framework's debate structure fosters a balanced reasoning process between exploring various perspectives and exploiting the known priors, towards achieving the complex, intricate capabilities required for AGI.

The contributions of this chapter are:

1. EVINCE *Framework Design*: Unlike approaches that use de-

bate merely to improve accuracy via redundancy, EVINCE facilitates information discovery, bias mitigation, and decision-making that requires both breadth and depth of information.

2. *Theoretical Foundations*: EVINCE establishes a theoretical basis for SocraSynth, rooted in conditional Bayesian statistics, mutual information, and dual entropy. These principles are applied to measure, monitor, and modulate collaborative LLM interactions, contributing to a deeper understanding of how LLMs can effectively cooperate for improved decision-making. The dual entropy theory is novel and ground-breaking, illustrating how a productive decision-making process should start with room for diverse input and stable objectives, and then, through information exchange, converge to optimal decision/prediction.

3. *Empirical Validation*: We provide empirical validation of the underlying theories of EVINCE, highlighting the framework's effectiveness in balancing exploration and exploitation to enhance prediction accuracy. We also introduce a set of maxims derived from our empirical findings, offering practical guidance for optimizing mutual information and minimizing various divergence measures.

8 Uncovering Errors and Biases with Reflective Large Language Models

Abstract Biases inherent in human endeavors pose significant challenges for machine learning, particularly in supervised learning that relies on potentially biased "ground truth" data. This reliance, coupled with models' tendency to generalize based on statistical maximum likelihood, can propagate and amplify biases, exacerbating societal issues. To address this, our study proposes a reflective methodology utilizing multiple Large Language Models (LLMs) engaged in a dynamic dialogue to uncover diverse perspectives. By leveraging in-context learning, information theory, and divergence metrics, this novel approach fosters context-dependent linguistic behaviors, promoting unbiased outputs. Furthermore, it enables measurable progress tracking and explainable remediation actions to address identified biases.

Introduction

Errors and biases in human-labeled data present critical challenges for machine learning models, especially in healthcare, news, education, and public policy, where their outputs can profoundly shape public perception and decision-making [148]. Errors, such as diagnostic mistakes, arise from knowledge gaps or lack of expertise, while biases, including ideological and societal distortions, can be consciously or unconsciously introduced by annotators. These flaws compromise the integrity of ground truth data, propagating through machine learning pipelines and generating undesirable outcomes [149, 150, 151].

AI systems are particularly vulnerable to these flaws, as models trained on inaccurate or biased ground truth data tend to replicate and amplify these issues through maximum likelihood estimation. In healthcare, diagnostic errors can lead to poor treatment recommendations [13], while in news, partisan annotations—such as labeling a biased article as neutral—mislead both human readers and automated classifiers, distorting public discourse [148, 152]. The impact extends beyond individual sectors: in education, biased data can reinforce stereotypes, while in public policy, it can result in discriminatory decisions. Ensuring that models learn from accurate and impartial ground truth data is therefore essential to the responsible deployment of AI across all domains.

This chapter focuses on bias detection and correction in news annotations, using news as the testbed to explore how reflective dialogues among LLMs can mitigate biases. News content is particularly vulnerable to ideological biases, as annotators' personal views often shape the interpretation of politically sensitive topics. Real-world evidence shows how annotation practices differ based on political affiliation. Real data illustrate that Democratic-leaning annotators may judge scandals involving Democrats more harshly than Republicans, and vice versa, highlighting the need for tools to balance these biases.

To address these challenges, we introduce the Reflective LLM Dialogue Framework (RLDF), which implements checks and balances using multiple LLM instances in structured dialogues. RLDF conditions two instances to take opposing stances: one supports the original label, while the other introduces alternative perspectives. These reflective exchanges foster deeper insights and help uncover potential biases, generating more neutral annotations through the inclusion of diverse viewpoints. This multi-LLM dialogue approach outperforms the results of a single LLM operating in isolation or providing one-off responses.

RLDF employs conditional statistics, information theory, and divergence metrics to measure the effectiveness of these dialogues. Shannon entropy [153] quantifies the diversity of perspectives, while mutual information [154] measures the quality of the exchange. To track the convergence toward unbiased outcomes, we apply Jensen-Shannon divergence (JSD) [155], Wasserstein distance (WD) [156], and cross-entropy (CE) [157], ensuring that the remediation actions are measurable and transparent for further refinement by human reviewers.

Our empirical studies validate the effectiveness of RLDF, and the contributions of this chapter are summarized as follows:

1. Adversarial and Reflective Inspection Framework: RLDF provides a structured framework that encourages adversarial and reflective inspection of ground-truth labels. Through dialogue, participating LLM instances examine, challenge, and explain biases embedded in the original annotations by offering various perspectives. For example, in news annotation, RLDF reveals hidden ideological biases by generating alternative interpretations for politically sensitive content, leading to more neutral labeling.

2. Careful Modulation of Linguistic Behaviors for Balanced Exploration and Exploitation: The effectiveness of RLDF lies in its

careful modulation of linguistic behaviors among participating LLM instances, alternating between contentious and conciliatory interactions. This dynamic trade-off fosters exploration of new perspectives while consolidating well-supported viewpoints. Information-theoretic and statistical metrics, including Shannon entropy, mutual information, Jensen-Shannon divergence, Wasserstein distance, and cross-entropy, are employed to measure opinion diversity, information flow, and the strength of the final assessment.

3. Effective Results and Impact on Improving Labels and Mitigating AI Bias: RLDF successfully mitigates AI biases, ensuring more reliable and unbiased model outputs across domains such as news, healthcare [6], and public policy. These outcomes demonstrate RLDF's significant impact in refining labels, enhancing fairness, and promoting responsible AI deployment.

9 Modeling Emotions in Multimodal LLMs

Abstract

In human-computer interaction, recognizing and responding to a user's emotional state is crucial for effective communication and successful task completion. For instance, a caregiving AI agent capable of detecting pain or depression in a patient could offer tailored empathetic support and appropriate medical interventions while adhering to ethical guidelines and safeguarding patient well-being. This chapter examines cognitive research on human emotions and proposes the Behavioral Emotion Analysis Model (BEAM), a novel emotion spectrum framework that incorporates both basic emotions and their linguistic antonyms. BEAM provides a comprehensive way to understand and represent emotional states in language and is designed to be integrated with Large Language Models (LLMs). By leveraging BEAM, LLMs can adapt their linguistic behaviors and expressions based on the detected emotional state of the user, ensuring responses are both empathetic and ethically aligned.

Introduction

During the development of SocraSynth [4], a multi-LLM debate framework, we discovered a fundamental principle about Large

Language Model (LLM) behavior. While investigating how to control debate "contentiousness," we found that an LLM's linguistic behavior could be systematically altered through emotional conditioning. High contentiousness produced confrontational tones and polarized language, while low contentiousness led to agreeable, considerate discourse. This observation went beyond the original scope of improving multi-agent debates—it revealed a mechanism for steering LLM behavior through emotional states.

Most multi-agent debate (MAD) systems [158, 144, 159, 160, 145, 143, 161] function as ensemble learning techniques, similar to bagging [162] or mixtures of experts [142], where LLMs simply exchange ideas without deep exploration. Our work with SocraSynth and EVINCE [6] addressed this limitation by dynamically modulating emotional states throughout the debate. High contentiousness drives LLMs to explore novel perspectives and challenge existing viewpoints, while low contentiousness promotes the synthesis of established ideas. This emotional modulation creates a natural debate progression: from vigorous exploration of diverse viewpoints, through reasoned analysis and refutation, to the emergence of well-examined, conciliatory conclusions.

While LLM training is often viewed simply as next-token prediction, its effects are far more profound. Training documents represent humans pursuing diverse goals—conducting research, exchanging opinions, expressing emotions—through a vast array of linguistic behaviors. This understanding, combined with our experience in modeling contentiousness through in-context learning, suggests an intriguing possibility: can we condition LLMs with specific goals and emotions to generate outputs that leverage these learned linguistic behaviors? Recent empirical studies support this approach, showing that LLM outputs can be traced to their source

[163] and that in-context learning operates as conditional statistics in a Bayesian framework [164].

Our exploration through bias reduction work in news articles and Wikipedia content [165] demonstrated that emotional states significantly influence LLM outputs. This finding, combined with our debate framework experiences, suggests that a mathematical model of emotions could provide a foundation for systematic behavior control. Before exploring the mapping between emotions and behaviors in the next chapter, we must first establish a rigorous framework for representing and manipulating basic emotions.

To lay the groundwork for emotion-based behavior control, this chapter develops the Behavioral Emotion Analysis Model (BEAM) [26]. While LLMs were initially seen as "black boxes" [106], our observations, along with insights from Prof. Stuart Russell, suggest that emotional states can be systematically modeled and conveyed to LLMs via *context*. Our model addresses three fundamental questions:

1. *What basic emotions form a complete basis?* We identify k fundamental emotion spectra, each defined by negative and positive antonyms (e.g., "hate-love", "anxiety-calmness"). We focus on basic emotions while excluding complex emotions like "regret" that arise from combinations of basic states. Each spectrum represents a continuous axis along which emotional states can be measured and modified.

2. *How can we mathematically manipulate emotions?* We develop a mathematical framework using negation and scaling operations for precise positioning of emotional states along each spectrum. For instance, given the hate-love spectrum, we can represent intermediate states through scaling (e.g., $0.7 \times$ love) and use negation to move between opposing states

(e.g., $\neg$hate $\approx$ love). These operations provide the foundation for systematic emotion manipulation.

3. *Can emotions predict behaviors?* We conduct a preliminary study using self-supervised learning to explore the relationship between emotional states and linguistic behaviors. By analyzing text samples from our debate framework, we train a model to predict behavioral patterns from emotional states without explicit labeling. This study validates our emotional spectra's utility in modeling behavioral outcomes while providing insights for more comprehensive behavior mapping in [7].

While the next chapter will explore how these emotional states map to specific linguistic behaviors in depth, this chapter focuses on establishing the mathematical framework for representing and manipulating basic emotions, validated through preliminary self-supervised learning experiments. By grounding our model in both mathematical rigor and empirical testing, we create a foundation for systematic emotion-based behavior control in LLMs.

10 A Checks-and-Balances Framework for Context-Aware Ethical Alignment of Large Language Models

Abstract This chapter introduces a three-branch checks-and-balances framework for ethical alignment of Large Language Models (LLMs). Inspired by governmental systems, the framework implements three independent yet interacting components: LLMs as the executive branch for knowledge generation, DIKE (named after the goddess of justice) as the legislative branch establishing ethical guardrails, and ERIS (the goddess of discord) as the judicial branch for contextual interpretation. The DIKE-ERIS duality, through their adversarial interaction, enables adaptation to diverse cultural contexts while maintaining consistent ethical principles. This architecture addresses fundamental limitations of reinforcement learning with human feedback (RLHF) by providing interpretable, adaptable, and culturally-aware ethical reasoning. Through self-supervised learning and adversarial testing, our framework demonstrates how emotional modeling can guide linguistic behaviors toward ethical outcomes while preserving the independence of knowledge generation, ethical oversight, and contextual interpretation.

11 ALAS: An Adaptive Multi-Agent System for Mitigating LLM Planning Limitations

Abstract

Large-scale Language Models (LLMs) face significant challenges in complex planning, particularly in reactive adaptation to dynamic conditions. Key limitations include inability to maintain temporal-spatial awareness during disruptions, lack of self-validation capabilities, and compounding errors in multi-step reasoning. This work introduces ALAS (Adaptive Learning Agent System), a multi-agent framework designed to overcome these challenges through continuous state tracking and robust reactive planning. ALAS employs independent validation agents, specialized domain experts, and hierarchical monitoring to maintain precise awareness of partially completed actions and generate physically feasible adaptations when conditions change—unlike traditional LLMs that attempt to "rewrite" history. Evaluations in multiple real-world scenarios demonstrate that architectural innovation in state tracking and reactive planning, rather than mere scaling, is the key to advancing AI planning capabilities, with ALAS achieving significant improvements in planning reliability and adaptation performance.

12 SagaLLM: Persistent Context Management, Constraint Validation, and Transaction Guarantees

Abstract

This paper introduces SagaLLM, a structured multi-agent architecture designed specifically to address four fundamental limitations of current LLM-based approaches: inadequate self-validation, context narrowing, absence of robust transaction-like guarantees, and insufficient inter-agent coordination. Unlike traditional MAS, current LLM approaches often lack critical safeguards such as transaction semantics, leading to unreliable execution and inconsistent states. To mitigate these challenges, SagaLLM integrates specialized context-management agents, compensatory rollback mechanisms, and rigorous independent validation protocols. Although it relaxes strict ACID constraints, particularly atomicity and isolation, SagaLLM adopts and adapts principles from the Saga transactional model to ensure coherent rollback and state consistency throughout complex, distributed planning processes. This transactional inspired approach significantly improves the robustness, constraint awareness, and adaptability of multi-agent coordination, even in the face of disruptions. Evaluations highlight that current standalone LLM systems, despite impressive reasoning abilities, frequently struggle with maintaining global constraints during complex planning tasks, particularly when adapting to unexpected changes. In contrast, the distributed transactional architecture of SagaLLM demonstrates significant improvements in planning consistency, constraint enforcement, and adaptive coordination during disruptions in diverse challenging scenarios.

13 Beyond Computation: Consciousness Modeling

Abstract The CoCoMo model proposes a computational solution to the challenge of incorporating ethical and emotional intelligence considerations into AI systems, with the aim of creating AI agents that combine knowledge with compassion. To reach this goal, CoCoMo focuses on fairness, beneficence, empathy, non-maleficence, adaptability, and critical and exploratory thinking abilities. CoCoMo employs consciousness modeling, reinforcement learning, and prompt template formulation to support these desired traits. By incorporating ethical and emotional intelligence considerations, a generative AI model can potentially lead to improved fairness, reduced toxicity, and increased reliability.

Introduction

Narrow AI, often referred to as System-1 AI following Kahneman's terminology [25], excels in executing well-defined, specific tasks through machine learning algorithms, including object recognition and language translation. However, this type of AI is not as effective in handling advanced generative AI functions that require reasoning, critical and exploratory thinking, or the modeling and regulation of emotions and behaviors. Such complex tasks go beyond the capabilities of System-1 AI, highlighting its limitations.

To address these limitations, researchers (e.g., Yoshua Bengio [166]) have proposed the development of system-2 AI, which aims to mimic human cognitive abilities. Several generative models have been developed since 2022 for text [115, 107, 108, 167], image [168, 169], and video generation [170]. However, these models face issues of bias, toxicity, robustness, and reliability [171, 172].

In this chapter, we propose a solution to address these concerns by modeling emotional intelligence and ethical guardrails within a generative AI model itself, drawing on insights from the study of human consciousness. We believe that addressing these issues outside of a generative AI model using human subjective feedback and reinforcement learning is equivalent to imposing censorship on user-generated content, which is a heuristic-based and non-scalable solution [173, 174].

Human consciousness is understood to manage both impulsive and reflective aspects of the unconscious, enabling compromises between competing goals and values. Emotions typically arise as impulsive reactions to stimuli, while ethics act as guardrails that help modulate or regulate emotion-steered motivations to sin. Developing a grasp of how human consciousness functions, not necessarily in physical terms but at least functionally, can offer vital insights for crafting a regulatory mechanism within a LLM. This mechanism would direct linguistic behavior and shape the linguistic features employed to achieve specific goals.

The nature and origin of consciousness have been studied for centuries, resulting in various theories, including the global workspace theory [175], integrated information theory [176, 177, 178], neural correlates of consciousness approach [179, 180], and attention schema theory [181, 182], among others. These studies of consciousness provide valuable insights for architecting system-2 AI.

This chapter defines system-2 AI's desired traits and capabilities using a functionalist approach to consciousness. These include knowledge, fairness, beneficence, non-maleficence, empathy, adaptability, transparency, and critical and exploratory thinking abilities. While this list is not exhaustive, it provides a starting point for developing ethical guardrails and emotional intelligence in AI systems. Depending on the context and application of AI, additional ethical considerations or modifications to these principles may be necessary.

To embody these capabilities and principles, we introduce the Computational Consciousness Model (CCM), which leverages priority-based scheduling, reward-based optimization, and Socratic dialogues. CCM offers customization based on cultural and individual requirements through adaptive prompt templates [5, 183], and facilitates the transition between unconsciousness and consciousness states through a multi-level feedback scheduler and interrupt mechanism.

To enable emotion and behavior modeling and regulation, as well as critical and exploratory thinking, CCM interacts with large language models[1] [115, 184, 107, 108, 167] using interactive question-answer-based dialogues. Furthermore, a reinforcement learning module maps external values and rewards to internal task-scheduling priorities.

CCM has the potential to support the development of adaptive computational consciousness that integrates knowledge and compassion, and models emotional intelligence for generative AI systems. This approach could significantly benefit humanity and society.

[1]Recent studies, such as [131], propose referring to these multimodal pretrained models as foundation models.

14 A Retrospective and Adaptive Framework to Improve LLMs

Abstract RAFEL is a retrospective and adaptive framework designed to benchmark private Large Language Models (LLMs) against teacher LLMs, identifying discrepancies in responses. Following the initial benchmarking, RAFEL categorizes these discrepancies into four distinct categories, based on cognitive levels and types of errors. Subsequent phases involve a detailed diagnosis and deep-probing to uncover the root causes behind each category of discrepancy. Teacher LLMs play a crucial role in interrogating the private LLM, shedding light on the subtleties of its performance issues. With a clear understanding of the symptoms and their underlying causes, RAFEL prescribes targeted remedies, accompanied by recommendations for relevant data sources to enhance the private LLM's performance via either fine-tuning, RAG, or both. Empirical studies validate RAFEL's effectiveness in diagnosing and enhancing the capabilities of localized LLMs.

Introduction

The emergence of Large Language Models (LLMs) like GPT [108] and Gemini [130] has significantly advanced the field of natural language processing, enabling the generation of text that closely mimics human writing and offers deep insights across varied domains. Despite their transformative potential, the deployment and scalability of these models pose considerable computational and data challenges. A practical response has been the fine-tuning of medium-sized, open-source models such as LLaMa [110] for specialized needs, allowing organizations to strike a balance between performance and feasibility, while also prioritizing data privacy and model customization for unique applications.

The shift towards using privately fine-tuned or locally deployed LLMs brings about essential management and technical challenges, vital for corporate strategy, governance, and innovation. This chapter explores the technical challenges of this shift, including:

- Justifying the choice of private LLMs over public counterparts by establishing relevant performance metrics and benchmarks for these specialized models.
- Conducting in-depth error analysis to pinpoint the root causes of performance issues in private LLMs, ensuring targeted and effective remediation strategies.
- Identifying specific, high-quality data crucial for the fine-tuning of private LLMs, aimed at enhancing their accuracy and domain relevance.
- Implementing Retrieval-Augmented Generation (RAG) to dynamically incorporate external, updated knowledge sources, improving the model's responsiveness and breadth of knowledge.
- Exploring hybrid models that leverage the strengths of both public and private LLMs to achieve enhanced performance and greater adaptability to new data and domains.

We introduce RAFEL, a framework designed for the retrospective and adaptive enhancement of LLMs, addressing these technical challenges. RAFEL strategically balances cost and performance by incorporating sophisticated diagnostic algorithms. These algorithms effectively identify and address the root causes of inefficiencies, ensuring that solutions are economically viable.

RAFEL employs advanced benchmarking metrics across cognitive levels, providing a thorough LLM performance assessment. Central to its diagnostics are two key algorithms: DIAG, for non-invasive[1] evaluation, and PRBE for thorough, invasive probing. This combination allows RAFEL to detect and understand both surface-level and deep-seated performance issues, facilitating targeted data source acquisition for enhancement.

RAFEL is proficient in creating targeted, effective remediation strategies, ensuring data privacy and security, validated through real-world data studies. The novelty claims of RAFEL include:

1. *Deep Probe with Cognitive and Error Type Analysis*: RAFEL goes beyond traditional error rate analysis by deeply probing into the LLM's responses, categorizing errors within cognitive levels (recollection, comprehension, analysis, reasoning) and types (hallucination, biases), enabling a deep understanding of the model's performance issues.

2. *Fine-grained, Precise Data Augmentation*: Contrasting with the conventional manual search for coarse-grained data augmentation, RAFEL identifies the required data and performs a more precise and relevant data enhancement that directly addresses the identified cognitive and error type deficiencies.

3. *Dynamic Remediation Playbook*: RAFEL dynamically adjusts its remediation strategy based on real-time analysis of data and errors, akin to adapting tactics in sports, ensuring the most

[1]Non-invasive methods evaluate without interacting with the LLM's internal data, whereas invasive methods directly engage with the LLM, accessing potentially sensitive data.

effective and appropriate intervention is applied.

15 Discovering Insights Beyond the Known

Abstract Human knowledge, vast as it is, often falls short in grasping intricate interdisciplinary domains fully. In contrast, foundation models like GPT-4, endowed with extensive multidisciplinary knowledge, can potentially bridge this gap. Significantly, we leverage the vast expanses of GPT-4's knowledge, banking on its ability to frame questions that might elude human intuition, thus paving the way for the emergence of fresh insights and potentially novel knowledge. In this study, we convened a unique committee comprising a moderator (the authors) and two GPT-4 agents. The dialogue is ignited by the ancient narrative of Adam and Eve, setting the stage for a rich exchange between the GPT-4 agents. This conversation derives from the age-old tale, as the agents investigate three intertwined domains: the significance of myths in ecological interpretation, the intricate ethical and philosophical quandaries surrounding AI, and the enigmatic realm of the human brain as complemented by technology. This dialogue not only unveils captivating insights but also underscores the indispensable value of interdisciplinary exchanges. Foundation models, as demonstrated, can catalyze such dialogues, equipping us to traverse expansive knowledge landscapes and explore domains previously beyond human comprehension.

Introduction

In our recent study on GPT-4 [106], we observed that GPT-4 along with analogous foundation models, manifests a *polydisciplinary* capacity [4]. (For clarity, we use "GPT-4" to collectively refer to these foundation models, given that our experiments are centered on GPT-4.) Trained on a vast spectrum of topics from varied sources, GPT-4 stands apart from human specialists. Such specialists, while deeply knowledgeable in their specific fields, often lack a broad understanding outside their particular domain. In contrast, GPT-4 processes knowledge without being tethered to domain boundaries. It doesn't compartmentalize a query strictly as a "physics question" or a "philosophy question," but crafts an integrated response, drawing from its multidisciplinary training data.

From a perspective of sheer knowledge breadth, GPT-4 arguably outpaces the average human. Its exposure to an enormous volume of documents endows it with a repository potentially wider than most human counterparts. However, volume isn't synonymous with depth. True depth often stems from intangible intuitions, insights, personal experiences, and cultural contexts. Considering GPT-4 lacks evolutionary experiences–ranging from survival instincts to the full spectrum of human emotions–we must ask: Can GPT-4 produce literature that deeply resonates with human sensibilities?

This study aims to ascertain if the polydisciplinary attributes of GPT-4 can generate insights that transcend standard human perspectives. We divide our research into two avenues: first, exploring the potential of GPT-4 to reveal "unknown unknowns," and second, assessing its aptitude for crafting emotionally impactful literature. This chapter examines the former, utilizing the universally recognized biblical tale of Adam and Eve and their consumption of the forbidden fruit as a common thematic foundation. Through this exploration, we aim to uncover viewpoints potentially beyond the realm of typical human cognition.

Our methodology revolves around orchestrating a dialogue between multiple GPT-4 agents. Within the experimental framework, a moderator (represented by the authors) sets the initial intent and context for the conversation. The number of participating agents and their underlying foundation models can be adjusted as needed. In this study, our committee consists of two agents based on the GPT-4 model, referred to as GPT-A and GPT-B. Once initialized, the agents engage in conversation autonomously, with minimal moderation (discussed shortly). The resultant dialogue is thoroughly analyzed to discern conversational patterns and depth of content. This in-depth examination facilitates the identification of diverse themes the GPT-4 model gravitates towards. Our underlying hypothesis posits that the discourse and exchanges between these agents can unearth insights–"unknown unknowns"–that were previously elusive to human understanding.

While the polydisciplinary capabilities of GPT-4 offer an unparalleled breadth and depth exceeding that of the moderator, the role of the moderator remains indispensable. This role channels the "exploratory" nature of the conversation, guiding it towards predefined objectives and ensuring its convergence within a set time frame. In this experiment, the initial spark for the dialogue is the narrative of Adam and Eve. Without prompting, the agents autonomously suggest probing the story from ten unique perspectives. Yet, after a series of exchanges, GPT-B expresses a keen interest in delving deeper. Following this, in collaboration with both agents, the moderator narrows down the scope of the dialogue to three key topics: ecological interpretation, philosophical exploration, and the neuroscientific angle. The intricate dialogues spanning these three domains–namely AI interwoven with Ecology, Neuroscience coupled with AI, and Neuroscience meshed with Ecology–are indeed engrossing. Throughout the discussion, both agents present a multifaceted perspective, shedding light on the diverse interpretations of the Garden of Eden, both prior to and following its seminal event. In the final stretch, the moderator verifies with both agents if they are poised to transition into the conclusion phase.

While our research unveils fascinating insights, it's essential to acknowledge several inherent limitations and constraints:

1. Model Training and Bias: GPT-4, akin to other machine learning models, is informed by pre-existing datasets. Therefore, the viewpoints, knowledge, and biases ingrained in this data can shape its outputs. It implies that GPT-4's responses might echo the historical and cultural biases present in the data upon which it was trained.

2. Interactivity Limitation: Conversations between two GPT-4 agents essentially access the same foundational knowledge. Consequently, while the discourse may encompass a range of viewpoints due to query processing, it won't yield wholly novel information. To glean potentially varied insights, it could be beneficial to facilitate dialogues between different iterations of GPT (like GPT-3 and GPT-4) or even entirely distinct foundation models such as LaMDA by Google and LLaMA by Meta AI.

3. Interpretation Subjectivity: Analysis of GPT-4's dialogues is susceptible to the prism of human interpretation. As such, different analysts might extract diverse conclusions from identical data sets.

We emphasize that the core intent of our study was experimental, rooted in the notion that a foundation model such as GPT-4 may offer knowledge both wider in scope and deeper in intricacy than most human capacities. While we've shed light on its potential strengths, we remain cognizant of the inherent risks and limitations. Our work's primary novelty lies in pioneering a discourse-driven approach with AI agents. Significantly, we leverage the vast expanses of GPT-4's knowledge, banking on its ability to frame questions that might elude human intuition, thus paving the way for the emergence of fresh insights and potentially novel knowledge.

16 Bibliography

[1] Edward Y. Chang. *Multi-LLM Agent Collaborative Intelligence: The Path to Artificial General Intelligence (First Edition)*. Amazon, 3 2024.

[2] Edward Y. Chang. *Multi-LLM Agent Collaborative Intelligence: The Path to Artificial General Intelligence (Third Edition)*. Amazon, 3 2025.

[3] Edward Y. Chang. CoCoMo: Computational Consciousness Modeling for Generative and Ethical AI. In *arXiv: 2304.02438*, 2023.

[4] Edward Y Chang. Examining GPT-4's Capabilities and Enhancement with SocraSynth. In *The* 10th *International Conf. on Computational Science and Computational Intelligence*, 12 2023.

[5] Edward Y. Chang. CRIT: Prompting Large Language Models With the Socratic Method. *IEEE* 13th *Annual Computing and Communication Workshop and Conference*, 3 2023.

[6] Edward Y Chang. EVINCE: Optimizing Adversarial LLM Dialogues via Conditional Statistics and Information Theory. In *arXiv:2408.14575*, 8 2024.

[7] Edward Y. Chang. A Three-Branch Checks-and-Balances Framework for Context-Aware Ethical Alignment of Large

Language Models. In *Advances in Neural Information Processing Systems, SafeGenAI Workshop*, 12 2024.

[8] Edward Y. Chang and Longling Geng. Sagallm: Context management, validation, and transaction guarantees for multi-agent llm planning, 2025.

[9] Immanuel Kant. *Critique of Pure Reason.* Cambridge University Press, Cambridge, 1781. Translated by Paul Guyer and Allen W. Wood, 1998.

[10] Friedrich Nietzsche. *The Will to Power.* Vintage Books, New York, 1968.

[11] Thomas Nagel. *The View from Nowhere.* Oxford University Press, 1986.

[12] Georg Wilhelm Friedrich Hegel. *Phenomenology of Spirit.* Oxford University Press, Oxford, 1807. Translated by A.V. Miller, 1977.

[13] David E. Newman-Toker, Kevin M. McDonald, Christopher J. Dy, and Linda T. Kohn. Serious Harm From Diagnostic Error in US Healthcare Systems: Estimate of Its Magnitude and Cost. *BMJ Quality & Safety*, 32(7):549–557, 2023.

[14] Edward Y. Chang. Uncovering Biases with Reflective Large Language Models. In *arXiv:2408.13464*, 2024.

[15] Nelson F. Liu, Kevin Lin, John Hewitt, Ashwin Paranjape, Michele Bevilacqua, Fabio Petroni, and Percy Liang. Lost in the middle: How language models use long contexts. *Transactions of the Association for Computational Linguistics*, 12:157–173, 2024.

[16] Youxiang Zhu, Ruochen Li, Danqing Wang, Daniel Haehn, and Xiaohui Liang. Focus directions make your language models pay more attention to relevant contexts, 2025.

[17] Howard Yen, Tianyu Gao, and Danqi Chen. Long-context language modeling with parallel context encoding, 2024.

[18] Kurt Gödel. On formally undecidable propositions of *Principia Mathematica* and related systems i. In Jean van Heijenoort, editor, *From Frege to Gödel: A Source Book in Mathematical Logic, 1879–1931*, pages 596–616. Harvard University Press, 1967. Translated by Jean van Heijenoort.

[19] Ludwig Wittgenstein. *Philosophical Investigations.* Macmillan, 1953. Translated by G.E.M. Anscombe.

[20] Karl Popper. *The Logic of Scientific Discovery.* Hutchinson, London, 1959.

[21] Alan Turing. Computing machinery and intelligence. *Mind*, 59(236):433–460, 1950.

[22] Erving Goffman. *The Presentation of Self in Everyday Life.* Anchor Books, New York, 1959.

[23] Sigmund Freud. The unconscious. *Standard Edition*, 14:159–215, 1915. Republished in 1957.

[24] David Eagleman. *Incognito: The Secret Lives of the Brain.* Pantheon Books, New York, 2011.

[25] Daniel Kahneman. *Thinking, Fast and Slow.* Farrar, Straus and Giroux, 2011.

[26] Edward Y. Chang. Behavioral Emotion Analysis Model for Large Language Models (invited paper). In *Proceedings of the* 7th *IEEE MIPR Conference*, August 2024.

[27] Sigmund Freud. *The Ego and the Id.* Standard Edition, Hogarth Press, 1923.

[28] Immanuel Kant. *Critique of Practical Reason.* Cambridge University Press (modern edition), 1788.

[29] Jean-Paul Sartre. *Being and Nothingness.* Washington Square Press, 1943.

[30] Michael S. Gazzaniga. *Who's in Charge? Free Will and the Science of the Brain.* Ecco, New York, 2011.

[31] Bernard J Baars. Global workspace theory of consciousness: toward a cognitive neuroscience of human experience. *Progress in Brain Research*, 150:45–53, 2005.

[32] Gregory Vlastos. *Socrates, Ironist and Moral Philosopher.* Cornell University Press, Ithaca, NY, 1991.

[33] Jocelyn J. Chang and et al. SocraHealth: Enhancing Medical Diagnosis and Correcting Historical Records. In *The* 10th *International Conf. on Computational Science and Computational Intelligence*, 12 2023.

[34] Aristotle. *Topics.* Oxford University Press, Oxford, 1928. Translated by W.A. Pickard-Cambridge, originally composed circa 350 BCE.

[35] Hannah Arendt. *The Human Condition.* University of Chicago Press, Chicago, 1958.

[36] Karl Jaspers. *Philosophy.* University of Chicago Press, Chicago, 1969. Translated by E.B. Ashton, originally published in German in 1932.

[37] Sigmund Freud. *The Interpretation of Dreams.* Macmillan, 1900.

[38] Flavie Waters, Angela Woods, and Charles Fernyhough. Hallucinations in schizophrenia and their relationship to duration of untreated psychosis. *Schizophrenia Research: Cognition*, 1:31–36, 2014.

[39] Maurice Merleau-Ponty. *Phenomenology of Perception.* Gallimard, 1945.

[40] Potsawee Manakul, Adian Liusie, and Mark JF Gales. Selfcheckgpt: Zero-resource black-box hallucination detection for generative large language models. In *Proceedings of the 2023 Conference on Empirical Methods in Natural Language Processing*, pages 12328–12344, 2023.

[41] Edward Y. Chang and Emily J. Chang. Discovering Insights Beyond the Known: A Dialogue Between GPT-4 Agents from Adam and Eve to the Nexus of Ecology, AI, and the Brain. In *Stanford InfoLab Technical Report*, 2023.

[42] Gilles Fauconnier and Mark Turner. *The Way We Think: Conceptual Blending and the Mind's Hidden Complexities.* Basic Books, 2002.

[43] David Silver, Aja Huang, Chris J Maddison, et al. Mastering the game of go with deep neural networks and tree search. *Nature*, 529(7587):484–489, 2016.

[44] David Silver, Julian Schrittwieser, Karen Simonyan, et al. Mastering the game of go without human knowledge. *Nature*, 550(7676):354–359, 2017.

[45] John Jumper, Richard Evans, Alexander Pritzel, et al. Highly accurate protein structure prediction with alphafold. *Nature*, 596(7873):583–589, 2021.

[46] Mariusz Bojarski, Davide Del Testa, Daniel Dworakowski, et al. End to end learning for self-driving cars. *arXiv preprint arXiv:1604.07316*, 2016.

[47] Jason Hawke, Alex Bewley, et al. End-to-end learning of driving models from large-scale video datasets. In *CVPR Workshops*, 2019.

[48] David G Lowe. Distinctive image features from scale-invariant keypoints. *International journal of computer vision*, 60(2):91–110, 2004.

[49] Alex Krizhevsky, Ilya Sutskever, and Geoffrey E Hinton. Imagenet classification with deep convolutional neural networks. *Communications of the ACM*, 60(6):84–90, 2012.

[50] Jiakai Liu, Rong Hu, Meihong Wang, Yi Wang, and Edward Y. Chang. Web-Scale Image Annotation. In *Advances in Multimedia Information Processing - PCM 2008*, pages 663–674. Springer, 2008.

[51] Zhiyu Wang, Dingyin Xia, and Edward Y. Chang. A deep-learning model-based and data-driven hybrid architecture for image annotation. In *Proceedings of the International Workshop on Very-Large-Scale Multimedia Corpus, Mining*

and Retrieval, VLS-MCMR '10, page 13–18, New York, NY, USA, 2010. Association for Computing Machinery.

[52] Edward Y. Chang. *Foundations of Large-Scale Multimedia Information Management and Retrieval: Mathematics of Perception.* Springer-Verlag, 2011.

[53] Andy Clark. Whatever next? predictive brains, situated agents, and the future of cognitive science. *Behavioral and Brain Sciences*, 36(3):181–204, 2013.

[54] Brenden M Lake, Tomer D Ullman, Joshua B Tenenbaum, and Samuel J Gershman. Building machines that learn and think like people. *Behavioral and Brain Sciences*, 40:1–70, 2017.

[55] Jared Kaplan, Sam McCandlish, Tom Henighan, Tom B. Brown, Benjamin Chess, Rewon Child, Scott Gray, Alec Radford, Jeffrey Wu, and Dario Amodei. Scaling laws for neural language models, 2020.

[56] Zellig S. Harris. Distributional structure. *WORD*, 10(2-3):146–162, 1954.

[57] George A Miller. Wordnet: a lexical database for english. *Communications of the ACM*, 38(11):39–41, 1995.

[58] Jia Deng, Wei Dong, Richard Socher, Li-Jia Li, Kai Li, and Li Fei-Fei. Imagenet: A large-scale hierarchical image database. In *2009 IEEE conference on computer vision and pattern recognition*, pages 248–255. Ieee, 2009.

[59] Susan T Dumais. Latent semantic analysis. *Annual review of information science and technology*, 38(1):188–230, 2004.

[60] David M Blei, Andrew Y Ng, and Michael I Jordan. Latent dirichlet allocation. *Journal of machine Learning research*, 3(Jan):993–1022, 2003.

[61] Tomas Mikolov, Kai Chen, Greg Corrado, and Jeffrey Dean. Efficient estimation of word representations in vector space, 2013.

[62] Jeffrey Pennington, Richard Socher, and Christopher D Manning. Glove: Global vectors for word representation. In *Proceedings of the 2014 Conference on Empirical Methods in Natural Language Processing (EMNLP)*, pages 1532–1543, 2014.

[63] Ashish Vaswani et al. Attention is all you need. *Advances in neural information processing systems*, 2017.

[64] Jacob Devlin, Ming-Wei Chang, Kenton Lee, and Kristina Toutanova. Bert: Pre-training of deep bidirectional transformers for language understanding, 2019.

[65] Sung-Hyuk Cha. Comprehensive Survey on Distance Similarity Measures between Probability Density Functions. 2007.

[66] Paul Jaccard. The distribution of the flora in the alpine zone. *New Phytologist*, 11(2):37–50, 1912.

[67] Anne M. Treisman and Garry Gelade. A Feature-Integration Theory of Attention. *Cognitive Psychology*, 12(1):97–136, 1980.

[68] Yann LeCun, Bernhard Boser, John S Denker, Donnie Henderson, Richard E Howard, Wayne Hubbard, and

Lawrence D Jackel. Backpropagation applied to handwritten zip code recognition. *Neural computation*, 1(4):541–551, 1989.

[69] Yann LeCun, Léon Bottou, Yoshua Bengio, and Patrick Haffner. Gradient-based learning applied to document recognition. *Proceedings of the IEEE*, 86(11):2278–2324, 1998.

[70] Max Wertheimer. Experimentelle studien uber das sehen von bewegung. *Zeitschrift fur psychologie*, 61:161–165, 1912.

[71] Kurt Koffka. *Principles of Gestalt Psychology.* Harcourt, Brace and Company, New York, 1935.

[72] Donald E. Broadbent. *Perception and Communication.* Pergamon Press, 1958.

[73] Baitao Li, E. Chang, and Ching-Tung Wu. DPF - A Perceptual Distance Function for Image Retrieval. In *Proceedings. International Conference on Image Processing*, volume 2, pages II–II, 2002.

[74] Beitao Li, Edward Y. Chang, and Yi Wu. Discovery of A Perceptual Distance Function for Measuring Image Similarity. *Multimedia Systems*, 8:512–522, 2003.

[75] Douglas L Medin, Robert L Goldstone, and Dedre Gentner. Respects for Similarity. *Psychological Review*, 100(2):254–278, 1993.

[76] R. L. Goldstone. Similarity, interactive activation, mapping. *Journal of Experimental Psychology: Learning, Memory, and Cognition*, 20(3):3–28, 1994.

[77] Alex Krizhevsky, Ilya Sutskever, and Geoffrey E. Hinton. Imagenet classification with deep convolutional neural networks. In *Proceedings of the 25th International Conference on Neural Information Processing Systems - Volume 1*, NIPS'12, page 1097–1105, Red Hook, NY, USA, 2012. Curran Associates Inc.

[78] D. H. Hubel and T. N. Wiesel. Receptive fields, binocular interaction and functional architecture in the cat's visual cortex. *The Journal of physiology*, 160(1):106–154, 1962.

[79] Kenneth A. Norman, Sean M. Polyn, Greg J. Detre, and James V. Haxby. Beyond mind-reading: multi-voxel pattern analysis of fmri data. *Trends in Cognitive Sciences*, 10:424–430, 2006.

[80] John-Dylan Haynes and Geraint Rees. Decoding mental states from brain activity in humans. *Nature Reviews Neuroscience*, 7:523–534, 2006.

[81] Allen Newell and Herbert A. Simon. Logic theorist and general problem solver. *Journal of the ACM (JACM)*, 1:256–260, 1956.

[82] Robert K. Lindsay, Bruce G. Buchanan, Edward A. Feigenbaum, and Joshua Lederberg. Applications of artificial intelligence for organic chemistry: The dendral project. *McGraw-Hill advanced computer science series*, 1979.

[83] Edward Hance Shortliffe, Bruce G. Buchanan, and Edward A. Feigenbaum. Mycin: A rule-based computer program for advising physicians regarding antimicrobial therapy selection. *AI in Medicine*, 10:199–208, 1975.

[84] William F. Clocksin and Christopher S. Mellish. *Programming in Prolog.* Springer-Verlag, 1981.

[85] J. Ross Quinlan. Induction of decision trees. *Machine Learning*, 1:81–106, 1986.

[86] I. T. Jolliffe. Principal component analysis. *Springer Series in Statistics*, 1986.

[87] Peter W. Foltz Thomas K Landauer and Darrell Laham. An introduction to latent semantic analysis. *Discourse Processes*, 25(2-3):259–284, 1998.

[88] Joshua B. Tenenbaum, Vin De Silva, and J. C. Langford. A global geometric framework for nonlinear dimensionality reduction. *Science*, 290:2319–2323, 2000.

[89] Laurens van der Maaten, Eric O. Postma, and Jaap van den Herik. Dimensionality Reduction: A Comparative Review. In *TiCC TR 2009–005*, 2008.

[90] Corinna Cortes and Vladimir Vapnik. Support-vector networks. *Machine Learning*, 20(3):273–297, 1995.

[91] David Barber. *Bayesian Reasoning and Machine Learning.* Cambridge University Press, 2012.

[92] Christopher M. Bishop. *Pattern Recognition and Machine Learning.* Springer, 2006.

[93] Andrew Gelman, John B. Carlin, Hal S. Stern, David B. Dunson, Aki Vehtari, and Donald B. Rubin. *Bayesian Data Analysis, Third Edition.* Chapman and Hall/CRC, 2014.

[94] Daphne Koller and Nir Friedman. *Probabilistic Graphical Models - Principles and Techniques.* The MIT Press, 2009.

[95] T.M. Mitchell. *Machine Learning.* McGraw-Hill series in computer science. McGraw Hill, 1997.

[96] Jeffrey Dean and Sanjay Ghemawat. Mapreduce: simplified data processing on large clusters. *Commun. ACM*, 51(1):107–113, 1 2008.

[97] Michael Cafarella, Edward Chang, Andrew Fikes, Alon Halevy, Wilson Hsieh, Alberto Lerner, Jayant Madhavan, and S. Muthukrishnan. Data management projects at google. *SIGMOD Rec.*, 37(1):34–38, 3 2008.

[98] Edward Y. Chang. *Foundations of Large-Scale Multimedia Information Management and Retrieval: Mathematics of Perception.* Springer, 2011.

[99] Edward Y. Chang, Kaihua Zhu, Hao Wang, Hongjie Bai, Jian Li, Zhihuan Qiu, and Hang Cui. Psvm: Parallelizing support vector machines on distributed computers. In *Proceedings of the 20th International Conference on Neural Information Processing Systems*, NIPS'07, page 257–264, 2007.

[100] Haoyuan Li, Yi Wang, Dong Zhang, Ming Zhang, and Edward Y. Chang. PFP: Parallel FP-Growth for Query Recommendation. In *ACM RecSys '08.* ACM, 2008.

[101] Yi Wang, Hongjie Bai, Matt Stanton, Wen-Yen Chen, and Edward Y. Chang. Plda: Parallel latent dirichlet allocation for large-scale applications. In Andrew V. Goldberg and Yunhong Zhou, editors, *Algorithmic Aspects in Information and Management*, pages 301–314, Berlin, Heidelberg, 2009. Springer Berlin Heidelberg.

[102] Wen-Yen Chen, Yangqiu Song, Hongjie Bai, Chih-Jen Lin, and Edward Y. Chang. Parallel Spectral Clustering in Distributed Systems. *IEEE Transactions on Pattern Analysis and Machine Intelligence*, 33(3):568–586, 2011.

[103] Z. Zheng, W. Jiang, G. Wu, and E. Y. Chang. Speedo: Parallelizing stochastic gradient descent for deep convolutional neural network. In *LearningSys, NeurIPS*, 2015.

[104] Artur d'Avila Garcez and Luis C. Lamb. Neurosymbolic ai: The 3rd wave, 2020.

[105] Lihui Lu, Qizhong Li, Jiyuan Liu, and Miaohua Huang. Combining domain knowledge and deep learning methods for vehicle trajectory prediction. *Journal of Physics: Conference Series*, 2303(1), 7 2022.

[106] Sébastien Bubeck, Varun Chandrasekaran, Ronen Eldan, Johannes Gehrke, Eric Horvitz, and more. Sparks of Artificial General Intelligence: Early experiments with GPT-4, 2023.

[107] OpenAI. Chatgpt, 2021.

[108] OpenAI. GPT-4 Technical Report, 2023.

[109] Romal Thoppilan, Daniel De Freitas, Jamie Hall, and et al. Lamda: Language models for dialog applications, 2022.

[110] Hugo Touvron, Louis Martin, Kevin Stone, and et al. Llama 2: Open foundation and fine-tuned chat models, 2023.

[111] Papers with Code Corp. Multi-task language understanding on mmlu, 10 2023.

[112] Long Ouyang, Jeff Wu, Xu Jiang, Diogo Almeida, Carroll L. Wainwright, Pamela Mishkin, Chong Zhang, Sandhini Agarwal, Katarina Slama, Alex Ray, John Schulman, and more. Training language models to follow instructions with human feedback, 2022.

[113] Jack Rae. Compression for AGI, Stanford MLSys, #76. `https://www.youtube.com/watch?v=dO4TPJkeaaU`, 2023.

[114] Jack W. Rae, Sebastian Borgeaud, Trevor Cai, Katie Millican, Jordan Hoffmann, Francis Song, and more. Scaling language models: Methods, analysis & insights from training gopher, 2022.

[115] Tom B. Brown, Benjamin Mann, Nick Ryder, and more. Language models are few-shot learners, 2020.

[116] Biyang Guo, Xin Zhang, Ziyuan Wang, Minqi Jiang, Jinran Nie, Yuxuan Ding, Jianwei Yue, and Yupeng Wu. How close is chatgpt to human experts? comparison corpus, evaluation, and detection, 2023.

[117] Thomas Wolf, Victor Sanh, Julien Chaumond, and Clement Delangue. Transfertransfo: A transfer learning approach for neural network based conversational agents, 2019.

[118] Chase B. Wrenn. Internet encyclopedia of philosophy, 2023.

[119] Wikipedia. Socratic method, 2023.

[120] Vladimir Dobrovolskii. Word-level coreference resolution. In *Proceedings of the 2021 Conference on Empirical Methods in Natural Language Processing*, pages 7670–7675, Online and Punta Cana, Dominican Republic, 11 2021. Association for Computational Linguistics.

[121] Panupong Pasupat and Percy Liang. Compositional semantic parsing on semi-structured tables. In *Proceedings of the 53rd Annual Meeting of the Association for Computational Linguistics and the 7th International Joint Conference on Natural Language Processing (Volume 1: Long Papers)*, pages 1470–1480. Association for Computational Linguistics, 7 2015.

[122] Li Dong and Mirella Lapata. Coarse-to-fine decoding for neural semantic parsing. In *Proceedings of the 56th Annual Meeting of the Association for Computational Linguistics*, pages 731–742. Association for Computational Linguistics, 7 2018.

[123] Plato. The republic.

[124] Linda Elder and Richard Paul. *The Thinker's Guide to the Art of Asking Essential Questions.* Rowman & Litterfield, 5th. edition, 2010.

[125] T. Airaksinen. Socratic irony and argumentation. *Argumentation*, 36:85–100, 2012.

[126] H. A. Stoddard and D. V. O'Dell. Would socrates have actually used the "socratic method" for clinical teaching? *Journal of general internal medicine*, 31(9):1092–96, 2016.

[127] M. N. Browne and S. Keeley. Asking the right questions, a guide to critical thinking, 2021.

[128] Richard Paul and Linda Elder. Critical thinking: The art of socratic questioning. *Journal of Developmental Education*, 31:34–35, 2007.

[129] Todd Thrash, Laura Maruskin, Scott Cassidy, James Fryer, and Richard Ryan. Mediating between the muse and the masses: Inspiration and the actualization of creative ideas. *Journal of personality and social psychology*, 98:469–87, 03 2010.

[130] Gemini Team, Rohan Anil, Sebastian Borgeaud, Yonghui Wu, Jean-Baptiste Alayrac, Jiahui Yu, Radu Soricut, Johan Schalkwyk, et al. Gemini: A family of highly capable multimodal models, 2023.

[131] Rishi Bommasani, Drew A. Hudson, and more. On the opportunities and risks of foundation models, 2022.

[132] Yifan Zhang, Jingqin Yang, Yang Yuan, and Andrew Chi-Chih Yao. Cumulative reasoning with large language models, 2023.

[133] Emilio Ferrara. Fairness and bias in artificial intelligence: A brief survey of sources, impacts, and mitigation strategies. *ArXiv*, abs/2304.07683, 2023.

[134] Otavio Parraga, Martin D. More, Christian M. Oliveira, et al. Fairness in deep learning: A survey on vision and language research. *ACM Comput. Surv.*, 12 2023. Just Accepted.

[135] Lei Huang, Weijiang Yu, Weitao Ma, Weihong Zhong, Zhangyin Feng, et al. A survey on hallucination in large language models: Principles, taxonomy, challenges, and open questions, 2023.

[136] Jie Huang and Kevin Chen-Chuan Chang. Towards reasoning in large language models: A survey. In *Findings of the*

Association for Computational Linguistics: ACL 2023, pages 1049–1065, 7 2023.

[137] Larry Page. The pagerank citation ranking: Bringing order to the web, 1998.

[138] Isaac Adams-Hands. Google algorithms: Decoding the secrets for improved search rankings, 2023.

[139] Edward Y. Chang. LLM Debate on the Middle East Conflict: Is It Resolvable? *Stanford University InfoLab Technical Report*, 10 2023.

[140] Wen-Kwang Tsao. Multi-Agent Reasoning with Large Language Models for Effective Corporate Planning. In *The* 10th *International Conf. on Computational Science and Computational Intelligence*, 12 2023.

[141] Edward Y Chang. SocraPedia: A Wikipedia Generated by SocraSynth with Collaborative Large Language Models. *Stanford University InfoLab Technical Report*, 11 2023.

[142] Robert A. Jacobs, Michael I. Jordan, Steven J. Nowlan, and Geoffrey E. Hinton. Adaptive Mixtures of Local Experts. *Neural Computation*, 3(1):79–87, 03 1991.

[143] Julian Michael, Salsabila Mahdi, David Rein, Jackson Petty, Julien Dirani, Vishakh Padmakumar, and Samuel R. Bowman. Debate helps supervise unreliable experts, 2023.

[144] Chi-Min Chan, Weize Chen, Yusheng Su, Jianxuan Yu, Wei Xue, Shanghang Zhang, Jie Fu, and Zhiyuan Liu. Chateval: Towards better llm-based evaluators through multi-agent debate, 2023.

[145] Tian Liang, Zhiwei He, Wenxiang Jiao, Xing Wang, Yan Wang, Rui Wang, Yujiu Yang, Zhaopeng Tu, and Shuming Shi. Encouraging divergent thinking in large language models through multi-agent debate, 2023.

[146] Yilun Du, Shuang Li, Antonio Torralba, Joshua B. Tenenbaum, and Igor Mordatch. Improving factuality and reasoning in language models through multiagent debate, 2023.

[147] Yoav Freund and Robert E. Schapire. A decision-theoretic generalization of on-line learning and an application to boosting. *Journal of Computer and System Sciences*, 55(1):119–139, 1997.

[148] Ninareh Mehrabi, Fred Morstatter, Nripsuta Saxena, Kristina Lerman, and Aram Galstyan. A survey on bias and fairness in machine learning. *ACM Computing Surveys (CSUR)*, 54(6):1–35, 2021.

[149] Jon Kleinberg, Sendhil Mullainathan, and Manish Raghavan. Inherent trade-offs in the fair determination of risk scores. *Proceedings of Innovations in Theoretical Computer Science (ITCS)*, 2017.

[150] Andrew D Selbst, Danah Boyd, Sorelle A Friedler, Suresh Venkatasubramanian, and Janet Vertesi. Fairness and abstraction in sociotechnical systems. In *Proc. of the Conference on Fairness, Accountability, and Transparency*, pages 59–68, 2019.

[151] Ricardo Baeza-Yates. Bias on the web. *Communications of the ACM*, 61(6):54–61, 2018.

[152] Sanjana Gautam and Mukund Srinath. Blind spots and biases: Exploring the role of annotator cognitive biases in nlp, 2024.

[153] Claude E. Shannon. A mathematical theory of communication. *Bell System Technical Journal*, 27(3):379–423, 1948.

[154] T. M. Cover and J. A. Thomas. *Elements of Information Theory*. John Wiley & Sons, 2 edition, 2006.

[155] Jianhua Lin. Divergence measures based on the shannon entropy. *IEEE Transactions on Information theory*, 37(1):145–151, 1991.

[156] Leonid V Kantorovich. On the translocation of masses. *Doklady Akademii Nauk*, 37(7-8):199–201, 1942.

[157] John E. Shore and Rodney W. Johnson. Axiomatic derivation of the principle of maximum entropy and the principle of minimum cross-entropy. *IEEE Transactions on Information Theory*, 26(1):26–37, 1980.

[158] Sahar Abdelnabi, Amr Gomaa, Sarath Sivaprasad, Lea Schönherr, and Mario Fritz. Cooperation, competition, and maliciousness: Llm-stakeholders interactive negotiation, 2024.

[159] Yao Fu, Hao Peng, Tushar Khot, and Mirella Lapata. Improving language model negotiation with self-play and in-context learning from ai feedback, 2023.

[160] Huao Li, Yu Chong, Simon Stepputtis, Joseph Campbell, et al. Theory of mind for multi-agent collaboration via large language models. In *Proceedings of the 2023 Conference on*

Empirical Methods in Natural Language Processing. Association for Computational Linguistics, 2023.

[161] Andries Smit, Paul Duckworth, Nathan Grinsztajn, Thomas D. Barrett, and Arnu Pretorius. Should we be going mad? a look at multi-agent debate strategies for llms, 2024.

[162] Leo Breiman. Bagging predictors. *Machine learning*, 24(2):123–140, 1996.

[163] Yushi Bai, Xin Lv, Jiajie Zhang, Hongchang Lyu, Jie Tang, et al. Longbench: A bilingual, multitask benchmark for long context understanding, 2023.

[164] Sang Michael Xie, Aditi Raghunathan, Percy Liang, and Tengyu Ma. An explanation of in-context learning as implicit bayesian inference. In *International Conference on Learning Representations (ICLR)*, 2021.

[165] Edward Y Chang. Uncovering Biases with Reflective Large Language Models. In *arXiv:2408.13464*, 8 2024.

[166] Yoshua Bengio. From system 1 deep learning to system 2 deep learning. *Neurips (Keynote)*, 2019.

[167] Romal Thoppilan, Daniel De Freitas, Jamie Hall, and more. Lamda: Language models for dialog applications. *arXiv*, abs/2201.08239, 2022.

[168] Aditya Ramesh, Prafulla Dhariwal, Alex Nichol, Casey Chu, and Mark Chen. Hierarchical text-conditional image generation with clip latents, 2022.

[169] Robin Rombach, Andreas Blattmann, Dominik Lorenz, Patrick Esser, and Björn Ommer. High-resolution image synthesis with latent diffusion models. *arXiv*, 2021.

[170] Uriel Singer, Adam Polyak, Thomas Hayes, Xi Yin, Jie An, and more. Make-a-video: Text-to-video generation without text-video data, 2022.

[171] Laura Weidinger, Jonathan Uesato, and Maribeth Rauh. Taxonomy of risks posed by language models. In *2022 ACM Conference on Fairness, Accountability, and Transparency*, FAccT '22, page 214–229, New York, NY, USA, 2022. Association for Computing Machinery.

[172] Terry Yue Zhuo, Yujin Huang, Chunyang Chen, and Zhenchang Xing. Exploring ai ethics of chatgpt: A diagnostic analysis, 2023.

[173] Jason A Gallo and Clare Y Cho. Social media: Misinformation and content moderation issues for congress, 2021.

[174] Jillian C. York. *Silicon Values: The Future of Free Speech Under Surveillance Capitalism.* Verso, 2021.

[175] Bernard J Baars. *A cognitive theory of consciousness.* Cambridge Univ. Press, 1988.

[176] Giulio Tononi. An information integration theory of consciousness. *BMC Neuroscience*, 5, 2004.

[177] Giulio Tononi. Integrated information theory. *Scholarpedia*, 10(1), 2015.

[178] Giulio Tononi. *Phi: A Voyage from the Brain to the Soul, Chapter 16.* Pantheon Books, 2012.

[179] Francis Crick and Christof Koch. Towards a neurobiological theory of consciousness. *Seminars in the Neurosciences*, 2(2):263–275, 1990.

[180] C. Koch. *The Quest for Consciousness: A Neurobiological Approach.* Roberts and Company, 2004.

[181] Michael Graziano. Attention schema theory: A mechanistic theory of subjective awareness. *Trends in cognitive sciences*, 20(8):588–600, 2016.

[182] Michael Graziano. *Consciousness and the social brain.* Oxford U., 2013.

[183] Pengfei Liu, Weizhe Yuan, Jinlan Fu, Zhengbao Jiang, Hiroaki Hayashi, and Graham Neubig. Pre-Train, Prompt, and Predict: A Systematic Survey of Prompting Methods in Natural Language Processing. *ACM Comput. Surv.*, 55(9), 1 2023.

[184] Renqian Luo, Liai Sun, Yingce Xia, Tao Qin, Sheng Zhang, and more. Biogpt: generative pre-trained transformer for biomedical text generation and mining. *Briefings in Bioinformatics*, 23(6), 09 2022.

Appendix X: Online Chapters

The following three chapters are available at SocraSynth.com.

SocraPlan: SocraSynth for Sales Planning

Abstract: SocraPlan introduces a sophisticated methodology that utilizes the capabilities of multiple Large Language Models (LLMs) for strategic sales planning in today's dynamic sales environment. This approach tailors sales playbooks to the unique needs and contexts of each customer by harnessing the power of Generative AI (GAI). Its primary objectives are to enhance customer satisfaction through a deep understanding of their specific requirements, refine sales strategies with targeted market analysis, and increase the efficiency of the sales process. SocraPlan sets itself apart with a collaborative and debate-driven framework that engages multiple LLMs, enabling a depth of analysis, adversarial reasoning, and strategy formulation that surpasses traditional AI-based approaches focused solely on data analytics. As a result, SocraPlan emerges as a pioneering tool in AI-driven sales strategies, delivering customized, effective solutions for complex sales planning challenges and facilitating more successful deal closures.

LLMs for Financial Planning and Analysis

Abstract: This paper elucidates the potential of leveraging large language models (LLMs) in the meticulous analysis of financial statements for the purpose of financial planning and analysis (FP&A). We commence by detailing a representative workflow encompassing the genesis of an FP&A report, inclusive of its structural outline and prerequisite data. This is succeeded by a delineation of the diverse data sources, which span primary financial statements, supplemental internal datasets, and external data from industry specific and governmental sources. Amid the diverse repertoire of reports within FP&A, we spotlight the generation of a "financial health assessment" report for a company as the focal point of our case study. Our methodology uniquely harnesses the strengths of LLMs, employing the ingenious Socratic Synthesis method to enhance the analysis and interpretative capabilities, thereby offering a more in-depth understanding of the data at hand. This approach not only accentuates the richness of the insights derived but also underscores the pivotal role of LLMs in advancing the realm of FP&A.

LLM Debate on the Middle East Conflict: Is It Resolvable?

Abstract: On October 7th, a renewed conflict arose between Israel and Palestine. Recognizing the historical significance and contentious nature of the Israel-Palestine conflict, this white paper engages two LLM agents in a debate over the question: "Is the conflict between Israel and Palestine resolvable?" A human moderator facilitates the discussion, intervening minimally. Through this debate, the paper seeks to highlight both the potential and constraints of contemporary LLMs.

Author's Biography

Edward Y. Chang has been an adjunct professor in the Computer Science Department at Stanford University since 2019. He previously served as the president of HTC DeepQ Healthcare (2012-2021), and as a director of research at Google (2006-2012), where he pioneered Web-scale image annotation (2008) and data-centric machine learning (2010), led initiatives in scalable machine learning, indoor localization, Google Q&A, and recommendation systems. He was a visiting professor at UC Berkeley (2017-2020), focusing on surgical planning with virtual reality. Chang was a tenured professor of Electrical & Computer Engineering at the University of California, Santa Barbara (1999-2006). He holds an MS in Computer Science and a PhD in Electrical Engineering, both from Stanford University. Beyond his technical education, he enrolled in more than ten courses in philosophy and literature, an intellectual breadth reflected in his publications.

Chang is a recipient of several awards, including the NSF Career award, Google Innovation award, US$1M XPRIZE (AI for disease diagnosis) and the ACM SIGMM Test of Time award. He is a Fellow of both ACM and IEEE for his contributions to scalable machine learning and healthcare.

ISBN: 978-1-962463-09-6 (Paperback)

Library of Congress Cataloging-in-Publication Data
Names: Edward Y. Chang, author.

Title: Unlocking the Wisdom of LLM Collaborative Intelligence
ISBN 978-1-962463-09-6 (Paperback)
Homepage: `http://infolab.stanford.edu/~echang`
Subjects: LCSH: Artificial Intelligence
Classification: LCC QA76.76.E95 | DDC 006.3–dc23
Imprint: SocraSynth.com (`http://socrasynth.com`)

Made in the USA
Monee, IL
08 November 2026

67994725R00094